HUMAN SHOWS
FAR PHANTASIES

SONGS, AND TRIFLES

BY

THOMAS HARDY

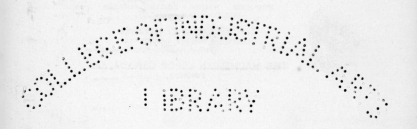
NEW YORK
THE MACMILLAN COMPANY
1925

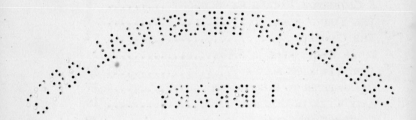

CONTENTS

CONTENTS

CONTENTS

CONTENTS

HUMAN SHOWS
FAR PHANTASIES

WAITING BOTH

A STAR looks down at me,
  And says: "Here I and you
Stand, each in our degree:
What do you mean to do,—
    Mean to do?"

I say: "For all I know,
Wait, and let Time go by,
Till my change come,"—"Just so,"
The star says: "So mean I:—
    So mean I."

A BIRD-SCENE.
AT A RURAL DWELLING

WHEN the inmate stirs, the birds re-
tire discreetly
From the window-ledge, whereon they
whistled sweetly
And on the step of the door,
In the misty morning hoar;
But now the dweller is up they flee
To the crooked neighbouring codlin-
tree;
And when he comes fully forth they seek
the garden,
And call from the lofty costard, as pleading
pardon
For shouting so near before
In their joy at being alive:—
Meanwhile the hammering clock within
goes five.

I know a domicile of brown and green,
Where for a hundred summers there have
been
Just such enactments, just such daybreaks
seen.

2

"ANY LITTLE OLD SONG"

ANY little old song
    Will do for me,
Tell it of joys gone long,
    Or joys to be,
Or friendly faces best
    Loved to see.

Newest themes I want not
    On subtle strings,
And for thrillings pant not
    That new song brings:
I only need the homeliest
    Of heartstirrings.

IN A FORMER RESORT
AFTER MANY YEARS

Do I know these, slack-shaped and
    wan,
Whose substance, one time fresh and
    furrowless,
Is now a rag drawn over a skeleton,
    As in El Greco's canvases?—
Whose cheeks have slipped down, lips
    become indrawn,
    And statures shrunk to dwarfishness?

Do they know me, whose former mind
Was like an open plain where no foot falls,
But now is as a gallery portrait-lined,
    And scored with necrologic scrawls,
Where feeble voices rise, once full-defined,
    From underground in curious calls?

4

A CATHEDRAL FAÇADE
AT MIDNIGHT

ALONG the sculptures of the western
    wall
    I watched the moonlight creeping:
It moved as if it hardly moved at all,
    Inch by inch thinly peeping
Round on the pious figures of freestone,
    brought
And poised there when the Universe was
    wrought
To serve its centre, Earth, in mankind's
    thought.

The lunar look skimmed scantly toe,
    breast, arm,
    Then edged on slowly, slightly,
To shoulder, hand, face; till each austere
    form
    Was blanched its whole length
    brightly
Of prophet, king, queen, cardinal in state,
That dead men's tools had striven to
    simulate;
And the stiff images stood irradiate.

5

A frail moan from the martyred saints
      there set
      Mid others of the erection
Against the breeze, seemed sighings of regret
      At the ancient faith's rejection
Under the sure, unhasting, steady stress
Of Reason's movement, making meaning-
      less
The coded creeds of old-time godliness.

THE TURNIP-HOER

OF tides that toss the souls of men
    Some are foreseen, and weathered
  warefully;
More burst at flood, none witting why or
    when,
    And are called Destiny.

—Years past there was a turnip-hoer,
Who loved his wife and child, and worked
    amain
In the turnip-time from dawn till day out-
    wore
    And night bedimmed the plain.

The thronging plants of blueish green
Would fall in lanes before his skilful blade,
Which, as by sleight, would deftly slip
    between
    Those spared and those low-laid.

'Twas afternoon: he hoed his best
Unlifting head or eye, when, through the
    fence,
He heard a gallop dropping from the crest
    Of the hill above him, whence,

Descending at a crashing pace,
An open carriage came, horsed by a pair:
A lady sat therein, with lilywhite face
    And wildly windblown hair.

The man sprang over, and horse and
    horse
Faced in the highway as the pair ondrew;
Like Terminus stood he there, and barred
    their course,
    And almost ere he knew

The lady was limp within his arms
And, half-unconscious, clutched his hair
    and beard;
And so he held her, till from neighbouring
    farms
    Came hinds, and soon appeared

Footman and coachman on the way:—
The steeds were guided back, now breath-
    bespent,
And the hoer was rewarded with good
    pay:—
    So passed the accident.

THE TURNIP-HOER 9

"She was the Duchess of Southern-
    shire,
They tell me," said the second hoe, next
    day:
"She's come a-visiting not far from here;
    This week will end her stay."

The hoer's wife that evening set
Her hand to a crusted stew in the three-
    legged pot,
And he sat looking on in silence; yet
    The cooking saw he not,

But a woman, with her arms around
    him,
Glove-handed, clasping his neck and clutch-
    ing his blouse,
And ere he went to bed that night he
    found him
    Outside a manor-house.

A page there smoking answered him:
"Her Grace's room is where you see that
    light;
By now she's up there slipping off her
    trim:
    The Dook's is on the right."

She was, indeed, just saying through
　　the door,
"That dauntless fellow saved me from
　　collapse:
I'd not much with me, or 'd have given him
　　more:
　　'Twas not enough, perhaps!"

Up till she left, before he slept,
He walked, though tired, to where her
　　window shined,
And mused till it went dark; but close
　　he kept
　　All that was in his mind.

"What is it, Ike?" inquired his wife;
"You are not so nice now as you used to
　　be.
What have I done? You seem quite tired
　　of life!"
　　"Nothing at all," said he.

In the next shire this lady of rank,
So 'twas made known, would open a
　　bazaar:
He took his money from the savings-bank
　　To go there, for 'twas far.

And reached her stall, and sighted, clad
In her ripe beauty and the goodliest guise,
His Vision of late.   He straight spent all he
    had,
      But not once caught her eyes.

Next week he heard, with heart of
    clay,
That London held her for three months or
    so:
Fearing to tell his wife he went for a day,
      Pawning his watch to go;

And scanned the Square of her abode,
And timed her moves, as well as he could
    guess,
That he might glimpse her; till afoot by
    road
      He came home penniless. . . .

—The Duke in Wessex once again,
Glanced at the Wessex paper, where he
    read
Of a man, late taken to drink, killed by a
    train
      At a crossing, so it said.

"Why—he who saved your life, I
   think?"
—"O no," said she.   "It cannot be the
   same:
He was sweet-breath'd, without a taint of
   drink;
   Yet it is like his name."

THE CARRIER

"THERE'S a seat, I see, still empty?"
    Cried the hailer from the road;
"No there is not!" said the carrier,
    Quickening his horse and load.

"—They say you are in the grave, Jane;
    But still you ride with me!"
And he looked towards the vacant space
    He had kept beside his knee.

And the passengers murmured: " 'Tis where
        his wife
    In journeys to and fro
Used always to sit; but nobody does
    Since those long years ago."

Rumble-mumble went the van
    Past Sidwell Church and wall,
Till Exon Towers were out of scan,
    And night lay over all.

LOVER TO MISTRESS

(SONG)

BECKON to me to come
        With handkerchief or hand,
Or finger mere or thumb;
Let forecasts be but rough,
Parents more bleak than bland,
        'Twill be enough,
            Maid mine,
        'Twill be enough!

Two fields, a wood, a tree,
Nothing now more malign
Lies between you and me;
But were they bysm, or bluff,
Or snarling sea, one sign
        Would be enough,
            Maid mine,
        Would be enough!

From an old copy.

14

THE MONUMENT-MAKER

I CHISELLED her monument
    To my mind's content,
Took it to the church by night,
When her planet was at its height,
And set it where I had figured the place in
    the daytime.
    Having niched it there
I stepped back, cheered, and thought its
    outlines fair,
    And its marbles rare.

Then laughed she over my shoulder as in
    our Maytime:
    "It spells not me!" she said:
"Tells nothing about my beauty, wit, or
    gay time
    With all those, quick and dead,
    Of high or lowlihead,
    That hovered near,
Including you, who carve there your de,
    votion;
    But you felt none, my dear!"

15

And then she vanished.   Checkless sprang
        my emotion,
            And forced a tear
At seeing I'd not been truly known by her,
And   never   prized!——that   my   memorial
        here,
        To consecrate her sepulchre,
            Was scorned, almost,
            By her sweet ghost:
Yet I hoped not quite, in her very inner-
        most!

1916.

CIRCUS-RIDER TO RINGMASTER

WHEN I am riding round the ring no
        longer,
    Tell a tale of me;
Say, no steed-borne woman's nerve was
        stronger
    Than used mine to be.
    Let your whole soul say it; do:
      O it will be true!

Should I soon no more be mistress found in
    Feats I've made my own,
Trace the tan-laid track you'd whip me
       round in
    On the cantering roan:
    There may cross your eyes again
      My lithe look as then.

Show how I, when clay became my cover,
    Took the high-hoop leap
Into your arms, who coaxed and grew my
       lover,—
    Ah, to make me weep
    Since those claspings cared for so
      Ever so long ago!

Though not now as when you freshly
            knew me,
        But a fading form,
Shape the kiss you'd briskly blow up to me
        While our love was warm,
    And my cheek unstained by tears,
        As in these last years!

LAST WEEK IN OCTOBER

THE trees are undressing, and fling
    in many places—
On the gray road, the roof, the
    window-sill—
Their radiant robes and ribbons and
    yellow laces;
A leaf each second so is flung at will,
Here, there, another and another, still and
    still.

A spider's web has caught one while
    downcoming,
That stays there dangling when the
    rest pass on;
Like a suspended criminal hangs he,
    mumming
In golden garb, while one yet green,
    high yon,
Trembles, as fearing such a fate for him-
    self anon.

COME NOT; YET COME!

(SONG)

IN my sage moments I can say,
    Come not near,
But far in foreign regions stay,
    So that here
A mind may grow again serene and clear.

But the thought withers. Why should I
    Have fear to earn me
Fame from your nearness, though
    thereby
    Old fires new burn me,
And lastly, maybe, tear and overturn me!

So I say, Come: deign again shine
    Upon this place,
Even if unslackened smart be mine
    From that sweet face,
And I faint to a phantom past all trace.

THE LATER AUTUMN

GONE are the lovers, under the bush
     Stretched at their ease;
     Gone the bees,
Tangling themselves in your hair as they
       rush
     On the line of your track,
     Leg-laden, back
     With a dip to their hive
     In a prepossessed dive.

Toadsmeat is mangy, frosted, and sere;
     Apples in grass
     Crunch as we pass,
And rot ere the men who make cyder
      appear.
     Couch-fires abound
     On fallows around,
     And shades far extend
     Like lives soon to end.

Spinning leaves join the remains shrunk
    and brown
    Of last year's display
    That lie wasting away,
On whose corpses they earlier as scorners
    gazed down
    From their aery green height:
    Now in the same plight
    They huddle; while yon
    A robin looks on.

"LET ME"

(SONG)

LET me believe it, dearest,
    Let it be
As just a dream—the merest—
    Haunting me,
That a frank full-souled sweetness
    Warmed your smile
And voice, to indiscreetness
    Once, awhile!

And I will fondly ponder
    Till I lie
Earthed up with others yonder
    Past a sigh,
That you may name at stray times
    With regret
One whom through green and gray times
    You forget!

AT A FASHIONABLE DINNER

WE sat with the banqueting-party
    By the table-end—
Unmarked,—no diners out
    Were we: scarce a friend
    Of our own mind's trend
Was there, though the welcome was
    hearty.
Then we noticed a shade extend
    By a distant screen,
And I said: "What to you does it seem to
    mean,
        Lavine?"

"—It is like my own body lying
    Beyond the door
    Where the servants glide in and
    about
    The carpeted floor;
    And it means my death hour!—"
"—What a fancy! Who feels like
    dying
    While these smart sallies pour,
    With laughter between!
To me it is more like satin sheen,
        Lavine."

"—That means your new bride, when
　　　you win her:
　　　Yes, so it must be!
It's her satin dress, no doubt—
　　　That shine you see—
　　　My own corpse to me!"
And a gloom came over the dinner,
Where almost strangers were we,
　　　As the spirit of the scene
Forsook her—the fairest of the whole
　　　thirteen—
　　　　　Lavine!

GREEN SLATES

(PENPETHY)

IT happened once, before the duller
 Loomings of life defined them,
I searched for slates of greenish colour
 A quarry where men mined them;

And saw, the while I peered around there,
 In the quarry standing
A form against the slate background there,
 Of fairness eye-commanding.

And now, though fifty years have flown
  me,
 With all their dreams and duties,
And strange-pipped dice my hand has
  thrown me,
 And dust are all her beauties,

Green slates—seen high on roofs, or lower
 In waggon, truck, or lorry—
Cry out: "Our home was where you saw
  her
 Standing in the quarry!"

AN EAST-END CURATE

A SMALL blind street off East
Commercial Road;
Window, door; window, door;
Every house like the one before,
Is where the curate, Mr. Dowle, has found
a pinched abode.
Spectacled, pale, moustache straw-coloured,
and with a long thin face,
Day or dark his lodgings' narrow doorstep
does he pace.

A bleached pianoforte, with its drawn silk
plaitings faded,
Stands in his room, its keys much yellowed,
cyphering, and abraded,
"Novello's Anthems" lie at hand, and also
a few glees,
And "Laws of Heaven for Earth" in a
frame upon the wall one sees.

He goes through his neighbours' houses as
    his own, and none regards,
And opens their back-doors off-hand, to
    look for them in their yards:
A man is threatening his wife on the other
    side of the wall,
But the curate lets it pass as knowing the
    history of it all.

Freely within his hearing the children skip
    and laugh and say:
    "There's Mister Dow-well!   There's
        Mister Dow-well!" in their play;
    And the long, pallid, devoted face
        notes not,
But stoops along abstractedly, for good, or
    in vain, God wot!

AT RUSHY-POND

ON the frigid face of the heath-hemmed
     pond
    There shaped the half-grown moon:
Winged whiffs from the north with a husky
     croon
    Blew over and beyond.

And the wind flapped the moon in its float
     on the pool,
    And stretched it to oval form;
Then corkscrewed it like a wriggling worm;
    Then wanned it weariful.

And I cared not for conning the sky above
    Where hung the substant thing,
For my thought was earthward sojourning
    On the scene I had vision of.

Since there it was once, in a secret year,
    I had called a woman to me
From across this water, ardently—
    And practised to keep her near;

Till the last weak love-words had been
    said,
    And ended was her time,
And blurred the bloomage of her prime,
    And white the earlier red.

And the troubled orb in the pond's sad
    shine
    Was her very wraith, as scanned
When she withdrew thence, mirrored, and
    Her days dropped out of mine.

FOUR IN THE MORNING

AT four this day of June I rise:
    The dawn-light strengthens steadily;
Earth is a cerule mystery,
As if not far from Paradise
          At four o'clock,

Or else in the Great Nebula,
Or where the Pleiads blink and smile:
(For though we see with eyes of guile
The grisly grin of things by day,
          At four o'clock

They show their best.) . . . In this vale's
    space
I am up the first, I think. Yet, no,
A whistling? and the to-and-fro
Wheezed whettings of a scythe apace
          At four o'clock? . . .

—Though pleasure spurred, I rose with
    irk:
Here is one at compulsion's whip
Taking his life's stern stewardship
With blithe uncare, and hard at work
                At four o'clock!

Bockhampton.

ON THE ESPLANADE

MIDSUMMER: 10 P.M.

THE broad bald moon edged up where
    the sea was wide,
    Mild, mellow-faced;
Beneath, a tumbling twinkle of shines,
    like dyed,
    A trackway traced
To the shore, as of petals fallen from a
    rose to waste,
    In its overblow,
And fluttering afloat on inward heaves of
    the tide :—
All this, so plain ; yet the rest I did not
    know.

The horizon gets lost in a mist new-wrought
    by the night :
    The lamps of the Bay
That reach from behind me round to the
    left and right
    On the sea-wall way

For a constant mile of curve, make a long
        display
    As a pearl-strung row,
Under which in the waves they bore their
        gimlets of light:—
All this was plain; but there was a thing
        not so.

Inside a window, open, with undrawn
        blind,
    There plays and sings
A lady unseen a melody undefined:
    And where the moon flings
Its shimmer a vessel crosses, whereon to
        the strings
    Plucked sweetly and low
Of a harp, they dance. Yea, such did I
        mark. That, behind,
My Fate's masked face crept near me I did
        not know!

IN ST. PAUL'S A WHILE AGO

SUMMER and winter close com-
   mune
On this July afternoon
As I enter chilly Paul's,
With its chasmal classic walls.
—Drifts of gray illumination
From the lofty fenestration
Slant them down in bristling spines that
      spread
Fan-like upon the vast dust-moted shade.

Moveless here, no whit allied
To the daemonian din outside,
Statues stand, cadaverous, wan,
Round the loiterers looking on
Under the yawning dome and nave,
Pondering whatnot, giddy or grave.
Here a verger moves a chair,
Or a red rope fixes there:—
A brimming Hebe, rapt in her adorning,
Brushes an Artemisia craped in mourning;

35

Beatrice Benedick piques, coquetting;
All unknowing or forgetting
That strange Jew, Damascus-bound,
Whose name, thereafter travelling round
To this precinct of the world,
Spread here like a flag unfurled:
Anon inspiring architectural sages
To frame this pile, writ his throughout the
ages:
Whence also the encircling mart
Assumed his name, of him no part,
And to his vision-seeing mind
Charmless, blank in every kind;
And whose displays, even had they called
his eye,
No gold or silver had been his to buy;
Whose haunters, had they seen him
stand
On his own steps here, lift his hand
In stress of eager, stammering speech,
And his meaning chanced to reach,
Would have proclaimed him as they
passed
An epilept enthusiast.

COMING UP OXFORD STREET :
EVENING

THE sun from the west glares
    back,
And the sun from the watered track,
And the sun from the sheets of glass,
And the sun from each window-
    brass;
Sun-mirrorings, too, brighten
From show-cases beneath
The laughing eyes and teeth
Of ladies who rouge and whiten.
And the same warm god explores
Panels and chinks of doors;
Problems with chymists' bottles
Profound as Aristotle's
He solves, and with good cause,
Having been ere man was.

Also he dazzles the pupils of one who
    walks west,
A city-clerk, with eyesight not of the best,

38 OXFORD STREET: EVENING

Who sees no escape to the very verge of
    his days
From the rut of Oxford Street into open
    ways;
And he goes along with head and eyes
    flagging forlorn,
Empty of interest in things, and wondering
    why he was born.

As seen July 4, 1872.

A LAST JOURNEY

"FATHER, you seem to have
    been sleeping fair?"
The child uncovered the dimity-curtained
    window-square
And looked out at the dawn,
    And back at the dying man nigh gone,
    And propped up in his chair,
Whose breathing a robin's "chink" took
    up in antiphon.

    The open fireplace spread
Like a vast weary yawn above his head,
Its thin blue blower waved against his
    whitening crown,
    For he could not lie down:
He raised him on his arms so emaci-
    ated:—

"Yes; I've slept long, my child. But
as for rest,
　Well, that I cannot say.
The whole night have I footed field and
turnpike-way—
　A regular pilgrimage—as at my best
　And very briskest day!

" 'Twas first to Weatherb'ry, to see
them there,
　And thence to King's-Stag, where
I joined in a jolly trip to Weydon-Priors
Fair:
　I shot for nuts, bought gingerbreads,
cream-cheese;
　And, not content with these,
I went to London: heard the watchmen
cry the hours.

" I soon was off again, and found me in
the bowers
　Of father's apple-trees,
And he shook the apples down: they
fell in showers,
Whereon he turned, smiled strange at me,
as ill at ease;
　And then you pulled the curtain; and,
ah me,
　I found me back where I wished not
to be!"

'Twas told the child next day: "Your
    father's dead."
    And, struck, she questioned, " O,
That journey, then, did father really
    go ?—
Buy nuts, and cakes, and travel at night
    till dawn was red,
And tire himself with journeying, as he
    said,
To see those old friends that he cared
    for so?"

SINGING LOVERS

I ROWED: the dimpled tide was at the
    turn,
And mirth and moonlight spread upon
    the bay:
There were two singing lovers in the stern;
    But mine had gone away,—
    Whither, I shunned to say!

The houses stood confronting us afar,
A livid line against the evening glare;
The small lamps livened; then out-stole
    a star;
    But my Love was not there,—
    Vanished, I sorrowed where!

His arm was round her, both full facing me
With no reserve. Theirs was not love to
    hide;
He held one tiller-rope, the other she;
    I pulled—the merest glide,—
    Looked on at them, and sighed.

The moon's glassed glory heaved as we
        lay swinging
Upon the undulations.   Shoreward, slow,
The plash of pebbles joined the lovers'
        singing,
      But she of a bygone vow
      Joined in the song not now!

Weymouth.

THE MONTH'S CALENDAR

TEAR off the calendar
     Of this month past,
And all its weeks, that are
Flown, to be cast
To oblivion fast!

Darken that day
On which we met,
With its words of gay
Half-felt regret
That you'll forget!

The second day, too;
The noon I nursed
Well—thoughts; yes, through
To the thirty-first;
That was the worst.

For then it was
You let me see
There was good cause
Why you could not be
Aught ever to me!

A SPELLBOUND PALACE

(HAMPTON COURT)

ON this kindly yellow day of mild low-
 travelling winter sun
   The stirless depths of the yews
   Are vague with misty blues:
Across the spacious pathways stretching
 spires of shadow run,
And the wind-gnawed walls of ancient
 brick are fired vermilion.

  Two or three early sanguine finches
   tune
 Some tentative strains, to be enlarged
   by May or June:
   From a thrush or blackbird
   Comes now and then a word,
While an enfeebled fountain somewhere
   within is heard.

   Our footsteps wait awhile,
   Then draw beneath the pile,
   When an inner court outspreads
   As 'twere History's own aisle,

Where the now-visioned fountain its at-
    tenuate crystal sheds
In passive lapse that seems to ignore the
    yon world's clamorous clutch,
And lays an insistent stillness on the place,
    like a cold hand's touch.

And there swaggers the Shade of a strad-
    dling King, plumed, sworded, with
    sensual face,
And lo, too, that of his Minister, at a bold
    self-centred pace:
Sheer in the sun they pass; and there-
    upon all is still,
Save the mindless fountain tinkling on
    with thin enfeebled will.

WHEN DEAD

TO ———

IT will be much better when
    I am under the bough;
I shall be more myself, Dear, then,
    Than I am now.

No sign of querulousness
    To wear you out
Shall I show there: strivings and stress
    Be quite without.

This fleeting life-brief blight
    Will have gone past
When I resume my old and right
    Place in the Vast.

And when you come to me
    To show you true,
Doubt not I shall infallibly
    Be waiting you.

SINE PROLE

(MEDIAEVAL LATIN SEQUENCE-METRE)

FORTH from ages thick in mystery,
   Through the morn and noon of
     history,
     To the moment where I stand
Has my line wound; I the last one—
Outcome of each spectral past one
     Of that file, so many-manned!

Nothing in its time-trail marred it:
As one long life I regard it
     Throughout all the years till now,
When it fain—the close seen coming—
After annals past all plumbing—
     Makes to Being its parting bow.

Unlike Jahveh's ancient nation,
Little in their line's cessation
     Moderns see for surge of sighs:
They have been schooled by lengthier
     vision,
View Life's lottery with misprision,
     And its dice that fling no prize!

TEN YEARS SINCE

'TIS ten years since
    I saw her on the stairs,
Heard her in house-affairs,
And listened to her cares;
And the trees are ten feet taller,
And the sunny spaces smaller
Whose bloomage would enthrall her;
And the piano wires are rustier,
The smell of bindings mustier,
And lofts and lumber dustier
    Than when, with casual look
    And ear, light note I took
    Of what shut like a book
    Those ten years since!

Nov., 1922.

EVERY ARTEMISIA

"YOUR eye-light wanes with an ail of
        care,
Frets freeze gray your face and hair."

    "I was the woman who met him,
        Then cool and keen,
        Whiling away
Time, with its restless scene on scene
        Every day."

"Your features fashion as in a dream
Of things that were, or used to seem."

    "I was the woman who won him:
        Steadfast and fond
        Was he, while I
Tepidly took what he gave, nor conned
        Wherefore or why."

"Your house looks blistered by a curse,
As if a wraith ruled there, or worse."

"I was the woman who slighted him:
      Far from my town
      Into the night
He went. . . . My hair, then auburn-
  brown,
      Pangs have wanned white."

"Your ways reflect a monstrous gloom;
Your voice speaks from within a tomb."

   "I was the woman who buried him:
      My misery
      God laughed to scorn:
The people said: ' 'Twere well if she
      Had not been born!' "

"You plod to pile a monument
So madly that your breath is spent."

   "I am the woman who god him:
      I build, to ease
      My scalding fires,
A temple topping the Deities'
      Fanes of my sires."

THE BEST SHE COULD

NINE leaves a minute
    Swim down shakily;
Each one fain would spin it
Straight to earth; but, see,
How the sharp airs win it
Slantwise away!—Hear it say,
"Now we have finished our summer show
Of what we knew the way to do:
Alas, not much!   But, as things go,
As fair as any.   And night-time calls,
    And the curtain falls!"

    Sunlight goes on shining
    As if no frost were here,
    Blackbirds seem designing
    Where to build next year;
    Yet is warmth declining:
And still the day seems to say,

"Saw you how Dame Summer drest?
Of all God taught her she bethought her!
Alas, not much!   And yet the best
She could, within the too short time
    Granted her prime."

Nov. 8, 1923.

THE GRAVEYARD OF DEAD
CREEDS

I LIT upon the graveyard of dead creeds
In wistful wanderings through old
wastes of thought,
Where bristled fennish fungi, fruiting
nought,
Amid the sepulchres begirt with weeds,

Which stone by stone recorded sanct,
deceased
Catholicons that had, in centuries flown,
Physicked created man through his long
groan,
Ere they went under, all their potence
ceased.

When in a breath-while, lo, their spectres
rose
Like wakened winds that autumn summons
up:—

54

"Out of us cometh an heir, that shall
    disclose
New promise!" cried they.   "And the
    caustic cup

"We ignorantly upheld to men, be filled
With draughts more pure than those we
    ever distilled,
That shall make tolerable to sentient seers
The melancholy marching of the years."

"THERE SEEMED A STRANGE-
NESS"

A PHANTASY

THERE seemed a strangeness in the
air,
Vermilion light on the land's lean face;
I heard a Voice from I knew not where:—
"The Great Adjustment is taking place!

"I set thick darkness over you,
And fogged you all your years therein;
At last I uncloud your view,
Which I am weary of holding in.

"Men have not heard, men have not seen
Since the beginning of the world
What earth and heaven mean;
But now their curtains shall be furled,

"And they shall see what is, ere long,
Not through a glass, but face to face;
And Right shall disestablish Wrong:
The Great Adjustment is taking place."

A NIGHT OF QUESTIONINGS

ON the eve of All-Souls' Day
    I heard the dead men say
Who lie by the tottering tower,
To the dark and doubling wind
At the midnight's turning hour,
When other speech had thinned:
  "What of the world now?"
The wind whiffed back: "Men still
Who are born, do good, do ill
Here, just as in your time:
Till their years the locust hath eaten,
Leaving them bare, downbeaten;
Somewhiles in springtide rime,
Somewhiles in summer glow,
Somewhiles in winter snow:—
     No more I know."

The same eve I caught cry
To the selfsame wind, those dry

As dust beneath the aisles
Of old cathedral piles,
Walled up in vaulted biers
Through many Christian years:
  "What of the world now?"
Sighed back the circuiteer:
"Men since your time, shrined here
By deserved ordinance,
Their own craft, or by chance,
Which follows men from birth
Even until under earth,
But little difference show
When ranged in sculptured row,
Different as dyes although:—
      No more I know."

On the selfsame eve, too, said
Those swayed in the sunk sea-bed
To the selfsame wind as it played
With the tide in the starless shade
From Comorin to Horn,
And round by Wrath forlorn:
  "What of the world now?"
And the wind for a second ceased,
Then whirred: "Men west and east,
As each sun soars and dips,
Go down to the sea in ships
As you went—hither and thither;
See the wonders of the deep,
As you did, ere they sleep;

But few at home care whither
They wander to and fro;
Themselves care little also!—
    No more I know."

Said, too, on the selfsame eve
The troubled skulls that heave
And fust in the flats of France,
To the wind wayfaring over
Listlessly as in trance
From the Ardennes to Dover,
  "What of the world now?"
And the farer moaned: "As when
You mauled these fields, do men
Set them with dark-drawn breaths
To knave their neighbours' deaths
In periodic spasms!
Yea, fooled by foul phantasms,
In a strange cyclic throe
Backward to type they go:—
    No more I know."

That night, too, men whose crimes
Had cut them off betimes,
Who lay within the pales
Of town and county jails
With the rope-groove on them yet,
Said to the same wind's fret
  "What of the world now?"

And the blast in its brooding tone
Returned: "Men have not shown,
Since you were stretched that morning,
A white cap your adorning,
More lovely deeds or true
Through thus neck-knotting you;
Or that they purer grow,
Or ever will, I trow!—
    No more I know."

XENOPHANES, THE MONIST OF COLOPHON

ANN: AET: SUAE XCII.—A: C: CCCCLXXX.

"ARE You groping Your way?
　　Do You do it unknowing?—
Or mark Your wind blowing?
Night tell You from day,
O Mover? Come, say!"
　　Cried Xenophanes.

"I mean, querying so,
Do You do it aware,
Or by rote, like a player,
Or in ignorance, nor care
Whether doing or no?"
　　Pressed Xenophanes.

"Thus strive I to plumb
Your depths, O Great Dumb!—
Not a god, but the All

61

(As I read) ; yet a thrall
To a blind ritual,"
    Sighed Xenophanes.

"If I only could bring
You to own it, close Thing,
I would write it again
With a still stronger pen
To my once neighbour-men!"
    Said Xenophanes.

—Quoth the listening Years:
"You ask It in vain;
You waste sighs and tears
On these callings inane,
Which It grasps not nor hears,
    O Xenophanes!"

"When you penned what you thought
You were cast out, and sought
A retreat over sea
From aroused enmity:
So it always will be,
    Yea, Xenophanes!

"In the lone of the nights
At Elea unseen,
Where the swinging wave smites
Of the restless Tyrrhene,
You may muse thus, serene,
    Safe, Xenophanes.

"But write it not back
To your dear Colophon;
Brows still will be black
At your words, 'All is One,'
From disputers thereon,
      Know, Xenophanes.

"Three thousand years hence,
Men who hazard a clue
To this riddle immense,
And still treat it as new,
Will be scowled at, like you,
      O Xenophanes!

" 'Some day I may tell,
When I've broken My spell,'
It snores in Its sleep
If you listen long, deep
At Its closely-sealed cell,
      Wronged Xenophanes!

"Yea, on, near the end,
Its doings may mend;
Aye, when you're forgotten,
And old cults are rotten,
And bulky codes shotten,
      Xenophanes!"

1921.

LIFE AND DEATH AT SUNRISE

(NEAR DOGBURY GATE, 1867)

THE hills uncap their tops
    Of woodland, pasture, copse,
And look on the layers of mist
At their foot that still persist:
They are like awakened sleepers on one
    elbow lifted,
Who gaze around to learn if things during
    night have shifted.

A waggon creaks up from the fog
With a laboured leisurely jog;
Then a horseman from off the hill-tip
Comes clapping down into the dip;
While woodlarks, finches, sparrows, try to
    entune at one time,
And cocks and hens and cows and bulls
    take up the chime.

With a shouldered basket and flagon
A man meets the one with the waggon,

And both the men halt of long use.
"Well," the waggoner says, "what's
    the news?"
"—'Tis a boy this time. You've just met
    the doctor trotting back.
She's doing very well. And we think we
    shall call him 'Jack.'

"And what have you got covered
    there?"
He nods to the waggon and mare.
"Oh, a coffin for old John Thinn:
We are just going to put him in."
"—So he's gone at last. He always had
    a good constitution."
"—He was ninety-odd. He could call up
    the French Revolution."

NIGHT-TIME IN MID-FALL

IT is a storm-strid night, winds footing
swift
    Through the blind profound;
  I know the happenings from their
    sound;
Leaves totter down still green, and spin
    and drift;
The tree-trunks rock to their roots, which
    wrench and lift
The loam where they run onward under-
    ground.

The streams are muddy and swollen; eels
    migrate
    To a new abode;
  Even cross, 'tis said, the turnpike-road;
(Men's feet have felt their crawl, home-
    coming late):
The westward fronts of towers are saturate,
Church-timbers crack, and witches ride
    abroad.

A SHEEP FAIR

THE day arrives of the autumn
    fair,
    And torrents fall,
Though sheep in throngs are gathered
    there,
    Ten thousand all,
Sodden, with hurdles round them
    reared:
And, lot by lot, the pens are cleared,
And the auctioneer wrings out his
    beard,
And wipes his book, bedrenched and
    smeared,
And rakes the rain from his face with the
    edge of his hand,
    As torrents fall.

The wool of the ewes is like a sponge
    With the daylong rain:
Jammed tight, to turn, or lie, or lunge,
    They strive in vain.

Their horns are soft as finger-nails,
Their shepherds reek against the rails,
The tied dogs soak with tucked-in
    tails,
The buyers' hat-brims fill like pails,
Which spill small cascades when they shift
    their stand
        In the daylong rain.

POSTSCRIPT

Time has trailed lengthily since met
        At Pummery Fair
Those panting thousands in their wet
        And woolly wear:
And every flock long since has bled,
And all the dripping buyers have sped,
And the hoarse auctioneer is dead,
Who "Going—going!" so often said,
As he consigned to doom each meek,
    mewed band
        At Pummery Fair.

SNOW IN THE SUBURBS

EVERY branch big with it,
  Bent every twig with it;
Every fork like a white web-foot;
Every street and pavement mute:
Some flakes have lost their way, and grope
    back upward, when
Meeting those meandering down they turn
    and descend again.
    The palings are glued together like a
      wall,
    And there is no waft of wind with the
      fleecy fall.

    A sparrow enters the tree,
    Whereon immediately
  A snow-lump thrice his own slight
      size
  Descends on him and showers his
      head and eyes,

69

And overturns him,
And near inurns him,
And lights on a nether twig, when
its brush
Starts off a volley of other lodging lumps
with a rush.

The steps are a blanched slope,
Up which, with feeble hope,
A black cat comes, wide-eyed and
thin;
And we take him in.

A LIGHT SNOW-FALL
AFTER FROST

ON the flat road a man at last appears:
　　How much his whitening hairs
Owe to the settling snow's mute anchorage,
And how much to a life's rough pilgrimage,
　　　One cannot certify.

　　The frost is on the wane,
And cobwebs hanging close outside the
　　pane
Pose as festoons of thick white worsted
　　there,
Of their pale presence no eye being aware
　　　Till the rime made them plain.

　　A second man comes by;
His ruddy beard brings fire to the pallid
　　scene:
　　　His coat is faded green;
　　　Hence seems it that his mien
　　　Wears something of the dye
Of the berried holm-trees that he passes
　　nigh.

The snow-feathers so gently swoop that
     though
        But half an hour ago
The road was brown, and now is starkly
     white,
A watcher would have failed defining
     quite
        When it transformed it so.

Near Surbiton.

WINTER NIGHT IN WOODLAND

(OLD TIME)

THE bark of a fox rings, sonorous
and long:—
Three barks, and then silentness;
"wong, wong, wong!"
In quality horn-like, yet melancholy,
As from teachings of years; for an
old one is he.
The hand of all men is against him, he
knows; and yet, why?
That he knows not,—will never know,
down to his death-halloo cry.

With clap-nets and lanterns off start
the bird-baiters,
In trim to make raids on the roosts in
the copse,
Where they beat the boughs artfully,
while their awaiters
Grow heavy at home over divers
warm drops.

73

The poachers, with swingels, and matches
     of brimstone, outcreep
To steal upon pheasants and drowse them
     a-perch and asleep.

    Out there, on the verge, where a path
      wavers through,
    Dark figures, filed singly, thrid quickly
      the view,
    Yet heavily laden: land-carriers are
      they
    In the hire of the smugglers from
      some nearest bay.
Each bears his two "tubs," slung across,
     one in front, one behind,
To a further snug hiding, which none but
     themselves are to find.

    And then, when the night has turned
      twelve the air brings
    From dim distance, a rhythm of
      voices and strings:
    'Tis the quire, just afoot on their long
      yearly rounds,
    To rouse by worn carols each house
      in their bounds;
Robert Penny, the Dewys, Mail, Voss,
     and the rest; till anon
Tired and thirsty, but cheerful, they home
     to their beds in the dawn.

ICE ON THE HIGHWAY

SEVEN buxom women abreast, and
   arm in arm,
     Trudge down the hill, tip-toed,
       And breathing warm;
They must perforce trudge thus, to keep
     upright
     On the glassy ice-bound road,
And they must get to market whether or
     no,
  Provisions running low
    With the nearing Saturday night,
While the lumbering van wherein they
     mostly ride
       Can nowise go:
Yet loud their laughter as they stagger
     and slide!

   Yell'ham Hill.

MUSIC IN A SNOWY STREET.

THE weather is sharp,
  But the girls are unmoved:
One wakes from a harp,
The next from a viol
A strain that I loved
When life was no trial.

The tripletime beat
Bounds forth on the snow,
But the spry springing feet
Of a century ago,
And the arms that enlaced
As the couples embraced,
Are silent old bones
Under graying gravestones.

The snow-feathers sail
Across the harp-strings,
Whose throbbing threads wail
Like love-satiate things.

Each lyre's grimy mien,
With its rout-raising tune,
Against the new white
Of the flake-laden noon,
Is incongruous to sight,
Hinting years they have seen
Of revel at night
Ere these damsels became
Possessed of their frame.

O bygone whirls, heys,
Crotchets, quavers, the same
That were danced in the days
Of grim Bonaparte's fame,
Or even by the toes
Of the fair Antoinette,—
Yea, old notes like those
Here are living on yet!—
But of their fame and fashion
How little these know
Who strum without passion
For pence, in the snow!

THE FROZEN GREENHOUSE

(ST. JULIOT)

"THERE was a frost
  Last night!" she said,
"And the stove was forgot
When we went to bed,
And the greenhouse plants
Are frozen dead!"

By the breakfast blaze
Blank-faced spoke she,
Her scared young look
Seeming to be
The very symbol
Of tragedy.

The frost is fiercer
Than then to-day,
As I pass the place
Of her once dismay,
But the greenhouse stands
Warm, tight, and gay,

While she who grieved
At the sad lot
Of her pretty plants—
Cold, iced, forgot—
Herself is colder,
And knows it not.

TWO LIPS

I KISSED them in fancy as I came
    Away in the morning glow:
I kissed them through the glass of her
   picture-frame:
       She did not know.

   I kissed them in love, in troth, in
     laughter
    When she knew all; long so!
That I should kiss them in a shroud
   thereafter
       She did not know.

NO BUYERS

A STREET SCENE

A LOAD of brushes and baskets
and cradles and chairs
    Labours along the street in the
    rain:
With it a man, a woman, a pony with
    whiteybrown hairs.——
    The man foots in front of the horse
    with a shambling sway
    At a slower tread than a funeral
    train,
    While to a dirge-like tune he chants
    his wares,
Swinging a Turk's-head brush (in a drum-
    major's way
    When the bandsmen march
    and play).

A yard from the back of the man is the
    whiteybrown pony's nose:
He mirrors his master in every item of pace
    and pose:

He stops when the man stops,
    without being told,
And seems to be eased by a pause;
    too plainly he's old,
        Indeed, not strength enough
        shows
    To steer the disjointed waggon
    straight,
Which wriggles left and right in a
    rambling line,
Deflected thus by its own warp and
    weight,
And pushing the pony with it in each
    incline.

    The woman walks on the pave-
        ment verge,
        Parallel to the man:
She wears an apron white and wide
    in span,
And carries a like Turk's-head, but more
    in nursing-wise:
        Now and then she joins in his
        dirge,
        But as if her thoughts were on
        distant things.
        The rain clams her apron till it
        clings.—
So, step by step, they move with
    their merchandize,
        And nobody buys.

ONE WHO MARRIED ABOVE HIM

"'TIS you, I think? Back from
your week's work, Steve?"

"It is I. Back from work this
Christmas Eve."

"But you seem off again?—in this
night-rime?"

"I am off again, and thoroughly off
this time."

"What does that mean?"

"More than may first be seen. . .

Half an hour ago I footed homeward
here,
No wife found I, nor child, nor maid,
indoors or near.

She has, as always, gone with them to her
　　mother's at the farm,
Where they fare better far than here, and,
　　maybe, meet less harm.
　　She's left no fire, no light, has cooked
　　me nothing to eat,
　　Though she had fuel, and money to get
　　some Christmas meat.
　　Christmas with them is grand, she
　　knows, and brings good victual,
　　Other than how it is here, where it's but
　　lean and little.
　　　　But though not much, and rough,
　　　　If managed neat there's enough.
　　She and hers are too highmade for
　　me;
　　But she's whimmed her once too often,
　　she'll see!
Farmer Bollen's daughter should never
　　have married a man that's poor;
And I can stand it no longer; I'm
　　leaving; you'll see me no more, be
　　sure.''

"But nonsense: you'll be back again ere
　　bedtime, and lighting a fire,
And sizzling your supper, and vexing
　　not that her views of supper are
　　higher.''

..

"Never for me."

"Well, we shall see."

The sceptical neighbour and Stephen then
      followed their foredesigned ways,
And their steps dimmed into white silence
      upon the slippery glaze;
And the trees went on with their spitting
      amid the icicled haze.

The evening whiled, and the wife with
      the babies came home,
But he was not there, nor all Christmas
      Day did he come.
Christmastide went, and likewise went
      the New Year.
But no husband's footfall revived,
And month after month lapsed, gray-
      time to green and to sere,
And other new years arrived,
And the children grew up: one hus-
      banded and one wived.—
      She wept and repented,
But Stephen never relented.
And there stands the house, and the
      sycamore-tree and all,
With its roots forming steps for the
      passers who care to call,

And there are the mullioned windows,
    and Ham-Hill door,
Through which Steve's wife was brought
        out, but which Steve re-entered
        no more.

THE NEW TOY

S HE cannot leave it alone,
    The new toy;
She pats it, smooths it, rights it, to show
    it's her own,
As the other train-passengers muse on its
    temper and tone,
    Till she draws from it cries of
    annoy:—
She feigns to appear as if thinking it
    nothing so rare
Or worthy of pride, to achieve
This wonder a child, though with reason
    the rest of them there
    May so be inclined to believe.

QUEEN CAROLINE TO HER GUESTS

D^{EAR} friends, stay!
    Lamplit wafts of wit keep
        sorrow
In the purlieus of to-morrow:
    Dear friends, stay!

Haste not away!
Even now may Time be weaving
Tricks of ravage, wrack, bereaving,
    Haste not away!

Through the pane,
Lurking along the street, there may be
Heartwrings, keeping hid till day be,
    Through the pane.

Check their reign:
Since while here we are the masters,
And can barricade dim disasters:
    Check their reign!

Give no ear
To those ghosts withoutside mumming,
Mouthing, threatening, "We are coming!"
Give no ear!

Sheltered here
Care we not that next day bring us
Pains, perversions!   No racks wring us
Sheltered here.

Homeward gone,
Sleep will slay this merrymaking;
No resuming it at waking,
Homeward gone.

After dawn
Something sad may be befalling;
Mood like ours there's no recalling
After dawn!

Morrow-day
Present joy that moments strengthen
May be past our power to lengthen,
Morrow-day!

Dear friends, stay!
Lamplit wafts of wit keep sorrow
In the limbo of to-morrow;
Dear friends, stay!

PLENA TIMORIS

THE lovers looked over the parapet-
        stone:
The moon in its southing directly blent
Its silver with their environment.
Her ear-rings twinkled; her teeth, too,
        shone
As, his arm around her, they laughed and
        leant.

A man came up to them; then one more.
"There's a woman in the canal below,"
They said; climbed over; slid down;
        let go,
And a splashing was heard, till an arm
        upbore,
And a dripping body began to show.

"Drowned herself for love of a man,
Who at one time used to meet her here,
Until he grew tired. But she'd wait him
        near,
And hope, till hopeless despair began.
So much for love in this mortal sphere!"

The girl's heart shuddered; it seemed as
    to freeze her
That here, at their tryst for so many a day,
Another woman's tragedy lay.
Dim dreads of the future grew slowly to
    seize her,
And her arm dropt from his as they
    wandered away.

THE WEARY WALKER

A PLAIN in front of me,
    And there's the road
Upon it.   Wide country,
    And, too, the road!

Past the first ridge another,
    And still the road
Creeps on.   Perhaps no other
    Ridge for the road?

Ah!   Past that ridge a third,
    Which still the road
Has to climb furtherward—
    The thin white road!

Sky seems to end its track;
    But no.   The road
Trails down the hill at the back.
    Ever the road!

LAST LOVE-WORD

(SONG)

THIS is the last; the very, very last!
   Anon, and all is dead and dumb,
Only a pale shroud over the past,
     That cannot be
   Of value small or vast,
     Love, then to me!

I can say no more: I have even said too
   much.
   I did not mean that this should come:
   I did not know 'twould swell to such—
     Nor, perhaps, you—
   When that first look and touch,
     Love, doomed us two!

189–.

93

NOBODY COMES

TREE-LEAVES labour up and
down,
And through them the fainting
light
Succumbs to the crawl of night.
Outside in the road the telegraph wire
To the town from the darkening
land
Intones to travellers like a spectral lyre
Swept by a spectral hand.

A car comes up, with lamps full-glare,
That flash upon a tree:
It has nothing to do with me,
And whangs along in a world of its
own,
Leaving a blacker air;
And mute by the gate I stand again alone,
And nobody pulls up there.

October 9, 1924.

IN THE STREET

(SONG)

ONLY acquaintances
        Seem do we,
Each of whom, meeting, says
        Civilly
"Good morning."—Yes: thus we appear
    to be!

But far, near, left and right,
        Here or there,
By day or dingiest night,
        Everywhere
I see you: one incomparably fair!

So do we wend our ways,
        Beautiful girl,
Along our parallel days;
        While unfurl
Our futures, and what there may whelm
    and whirl.

THE LAST LEAF

"THE leaves throng thick above:—
    Well, I'll come back, dear Love,
  When they all are down!"

She watched that August tree,
(None now scorned summer as she),
    Till it broidered it brown.

And then October came blowing,
And the leaves showed signs they were
      going,
    And she saw up through them.

O how she counted them then!
—November left her but ten,
    And started to strew them.

"Ah, when they all are gone,
And the skeleton-time comes on,
    Whom shall I see!"

—When the fifteenth spread its sky
That month, her upturned eye
    Could count but three.

And at the close of the week
A flush flapped over her cheek:
    The last one fell.

But—he did not come. And, at length,
Her hope of him lost all strength,
    And it was as a knell. . . .

When he did come again,
Years later, a husband then,
    Heavy somewhat,

With a smile she reminded him:
And he cried: "Ah, that vow of our
      whim!—
    Which I forgot,

"As one does!—And was that the tree?
So it was!—Dear me, dear me:
    Yes: I forgot."

AT WYNYARD'S GAP

SHE (*on horseback*)

THE hounds pass here?

HE (*on horseback*)

They did an hour ago,
Just in full cry, and went down-wind, I
saw,
Towards Pen Wood, where they may kill,
and draw
A second time, and bear towards the Yeo.

SHE

How vexing!   And I've crept along un-
thinking.

HE

Ah!—lost in dreams.   Fancy to fancy
linking!

SHE (*more softly*)

Not that, quite. . . . Now, to settle what
I'll do.

HE

Go home again.   But have you seen the
     view
From the top there?   Not?   It's really
     worth your while.—
You must dismount, because there is a
     stile.

*They dismount, hitch their horses, and
climb a few-score yards from the road.*

There you see half South Wessex,—combe,
     and glen,
And down, to Lewsdon Hill and Pilsdon
     Pen.

SHE

Yes.   It is fine.   And I, though living
     out there
By Crewkerne, never knew it.   (*She turns
     her head*) Well, I declare,
Look at the horses!—How shall I catch my
     mare?

*The horses have got loose and scampered
off.*

Now that's your fault, through leading me
     up here!
You must have known 'twould happen—

HE

No, my dear!

SHE

I'm not your dear.

HE (*blandly*)

But you can't help being so,
If it comes to that.   The fairest girl I've
    seen
Is of course dear—by her own fault, I
    mean.

SHE (*quickly*)

What house is that we see just down below?

HE

Oh—that's the inn called "Wynyard's
    Gap."—I'll go
While you wait here, and catch those brutes.
    Don't stir.

He goes.   She waits.

SHE

What a handsome man.   Not local, I'll
    aver.
He comes back.

HE

I met a farmer's labourer some way on;
He says he'll bring them to us here anon,
If possible before the day is dim.
Come down to the inn: there we can wait
    for him.

They descend slowly in that direction.

SHE

What a lonely inn.   Why is there such a
    one?

HE

For us to wait at.   Thus 'tis things are
    done.

SHE

Thus things are done?   Well—what things
    do you mean?

HE

Romantic things.   Meetings unknown, un-
    seen.

SHE

But ours is accident, and needn't have
    been,
And isn't what I'd plan with a stranger,
    quite,
Particularly at this time—nearly night.

HE

Nor I.   But still, the tavern's loneliness
Is favourable for lovers in distress,
When they've eloped, for instance, and are
     in fear
Of being pursued.   No one would find them
     here.

> *He goes to speak to the labourer ap-*
> *proaching; and returns.*

He says the horses long have passed the
     combe,
And cannot be overtaken.   They'll go
     home.

SHE

And what's to be done?   And it's begin-
     ning to rain.
'Tis always so.   One trouble brings a train!

HE

It seems to me that here we'd better stay
And rest us till some vehicle comes this
     way:
In fact, we might put up here till the
     morning:
The floods are high, and night-farers have
     warning.

SHE

Put up?   Do you think so!

HE

                        I incline to such,
My *dear* (do you mind?)

SHE

  Yes.—Well (*more softly*), I don't much,
If I seem like it.   But I ought to tell
     you
One thing.   I'm married.   Being so, it's
     well you—

HE

Oh, so am I.   (*A silence, he regarding her*)
     I note a charming thing—
You stand so stock-still that your ear-ring
     shakes
At each pulsation which the vein there
     makes.

SHE

Does it?   Perhaps because it's flustering
To be caught thus!   (*In a murmur*) Why
     did we chance to meet here?

HE

God knows!   Perhaps to taste a bitter-
        sweet here.—
Still, let us enter.   Shelter we must get:
The night is darkening and is growing wet.
So, anyhow, you can treat me as a lover
Just for this once.   To-morrow 'twill be
        over!

> *They reach the inn.   The door is locked,
> and they discern a board marked "To
> Let."   While they stand stultified
> a van is seen drawing near with
> passengers.*

SHE

Ah, here's an end of it!   The Crewkerne
        carrier.

HE

So cynic circumstance erects its barrier!

SHE (*mischievously*)

To your love-making, which would have
        grown stronger,
No doubt, if we had stayed on here much
        longer?

> *The carrier comes up.   Her companion
> reluctantly hails him.*

HE

Yes. . . . And in which you might have
    shown some ruth,
Had but the inn been open!—Well, for-
    sooth,
I'm sorry it's not. Are you? Now, dear,
    the truth!

SHE (*with gentle evasiveness*)

I am—almost. But best 'tis thus to be.
For—dear one—there I've said it!—you
    can see
That both at one inn (though roomed
    separately,
Of course)—so lone, too—might have been
    unfit,
Perfect as 'tis for lovers, I admit.

HE (*after a sigh*)
Carrier! A lift for my wife, please.

SHE (*in quick undertones*)
            Wife? But nay—

HE (*continuing*)
Her horse has thrown her and has gone
    astray:

See she gets safe to Crewkerne.   I've to
stay.

CARRIER

I will, sir!   I'm for Crookhorn straight
away.

HE (*to her, aloud*)

Right now, dear.   I shall soon be home.
Adieu!   (*Kisses her*).

SHE (*whispering confusedly*)

You shouldn't!   Pretending you are my
husband, too!
I now must act the part of wife to you!

HE (*whispering*)

Yes, since I've kissed you, dear.   You see
it's done
To silence tongues as we're found here
alone
At night, by gossipers, and seem as shown
Staying together!

SHE (*whispering*)

Then must I, too, kiss?

HE

Yes; a mere matter of form you know,
To check all scandal. People will talk so!

SHE

I'd no idea it would reach to this!
                              (*Kisses him*)
What makes it worse is, I'm ashamed to
        say,
I've a young baby waiting me at home!

HE

Ah—there you beat me!—But, my dear-
        est, play
The wife to the end, and don't give me
        away,
Despite the baby, since we've got so far,
And what we've acted feel we almost are!

SHE (*sighing*)

Yes. 'Tis so! And my conscience has
        gone dumb !

(*Aloud*)

'Bye, dear, awhile ! I'll sit up till you
        come.

(*In a whisper*)

Which means Good-bye for ever, truly
        heard !
Upon to-night be silent !

HE

                Never a word,
Till Pilsdon Pen by Marshwood wind is
        stirred !

He hands her up.   Exeunt omnes.

AT SHAG'S HEATH
1685

(TRADITIONAL)

I GRIEVE and grieve for what I have
　　done,
And nothing now is left to me
But straight to drown; yea, I have slain
The rarest soul the world shall see!
—My husband said: "Now thou art wed
Thou must beware!　And should a man
Cajole, mind, he means ill to thee,
Depend on't: fool him if ye can!"
　　But 'twas King Monmouth, he!

As truth I took what was not true:
Till darked my door just such a one.
He asked me but the way to go,
Though looking all so down and done.
And as he stood he said, unsued,
"The prettiest wife I've eyed to-day!"
And then he kissed me tenderly
Before he footed fast away
　　Did dear King Monmouth, he!

Builded was he so beautiful!—
Why did I pout a pettish word
For what he'd done?—Then whisking off—
For his pursuers' feet were heard—
"Dear one, keep faith!" he turns and saith,
And next he vanished in the copse
Before I knew what such might be,
And how great fears and how great hopes
     Had rare King Monmouth—he!

Up rode the soldiers. "Where's this
     man?—
He is the rebel Duke," say they.
"And calls himself King Monmouth, sure!"
Then I believed my husband; aye,
Though he'd spoke lies in jealous-wise!
—To Shag's nigh copse beyond the road
I moved my finger mercilessly;
And there lay hidden where I showed:
     My dear King Monmouth, he!

The soldiers brought him by my door,
His elbows bound behind him, fast;
Passing, he me-ward cast his eyes—
What eyes of beauty did he cast!
Grieved was his glance at me askance:
"I wished all weal might thee attend,
But this is what th'st done to me,
O heartless woman, held my friend!"
     Said sweet King Monmouth, he!

O then I saw he was no hind,
But a great lord of loftihood,
Come here to claim his rule and rights,
Who'd wished me, as he'd said, but good.——
With tug and jolt, then, out to Holt,
To Justice Ettricke, he was led,
And thence to London speedily,
Where under yester's headsman bled
    The rare King Monmouth, he!

Last night, the while my husband slept,
He rose up at the window there,
All blood and blear, and hacked about,
With heavy eyes, and rumpled hair;
And said: "My Love, 'twas cruel of
A Fair like thee to use me so!
But now it's nought: from foes I'm free!
Sooner or later all must go,"
    Said dear King Monmouth, he!

"Yes, lovely cruel one!" he said
In through the mullioned pane, shroud-
    pale,
"I love you still, would kiss you now,
But blood would stain your nighty-rail!"
——That's all. And so to drown I go:
O wear no weeds, my friends, for me . . .
When comes the waterman, he'll say,
"Who's done her thuswise?"——'Twill be,
    yea,
    Sweet, slain King Monmouth——he!

A SECOND ATTEMPT

THIRTY years after
       I began again
An old-time passion:
And it seemed as fresh as when
The first day ventured on:
When mutely I would waft her
In Love's past fashion
Dreams much dwelt upon,
Dreams I wished she knew.

I went the course through,
From Love's fresh-found sensation—
Remembered still so well—
To worn words charged anew,
That left no more to tell:
Thence to hot hopes and fears,
And thence to consummation,
And thence to sober years,
Markless, and mellow-hued.

Firm the whole fabric stood,
Or seemed to stand, and sound
As it had stood before.
But nothing backward climbs,
And when I looked around
As at the former times,
There was Life—pale and hoar;
And slow it said to me,
"Twice-over cannot be!"

"FREED THE FRET OF THINKING"

FREED the fret of thinking,
    Light of lot were we,
Song with service linking
    Like to bird or bee:
Chancing bale unblinking,
Freed the fret of thinking
    On mortality!

Had not thought-endowment
    Beings ever known,
What Life once or now meant
    None had wantéd shown—
Measuring but the moment—
Had not thought-endowment
    Caught Creation's groan!

Loosed from wrings of reason,
    We might blow like flowers,
Sense of Time-wrought treason
    Would not then be ours
In and out of season;
Loosed from wrings of reason
    We should laud the Powers!

114

THE ABSOLUTE EXPLAINS

I

"O NO," said It: her lifedoings
    Time's touch hath not destroyed:
They lie their length, with the throbbing
    things
    Akin them, down the Void,
        Live, unalloyed.

II

"Know, Time is toothless, seen all
    through;
    The Present, that men but see,
Is phasmal: since in a sane purview
    All things are shaped to be
        Eternally.

III

"Your 'Now' is just a gleam, a glide
    Across your gazing sense:
With me, 'Past,' 'Future,' ever abide:
    They come not, go not, whence
        They are never hence.

IV

"As one upon a dark highway,
        Plodding by lantern-light,
Finds but the reach of its frail ray
        Uncovered to his sight,
                Though mid the night.

V

"The road lies all its length the same,
        Forwardly as at rear,
So, outside what you 'Present' name,
        Future and Past stand sheer,
                Cognate and clear."

VI

—Thus It: who straightway opened then
        The vista called the Past,
Wherein were seen, as fair as when
        They seemed they could not last,
                Small things and vast.

VII

There were those songs, a score times sung,
        With all their tripping tunes,
There were the laughters once that rung,
        There those unmatched full moons,
                Those idle noons!

VIII

There fadeless, fixed, were dust-dead
     flowers
    Remaining still in blow;
Elsewhere, wild love-makings in bowers;
    Hard by, that irised bow
        Of years ago.

IX

There were my ever memorable
    Glad days of pilgrimage,
Coiled like a precious parchment fell,
    Illumined page by page,
        Unhurt by age.

X

"—Here you see spread those mortal ails
    So powerless to restrain
Your young life's eager hot assails,
    With hazards then not plain
        Till past their pain.

XI

"Here you see her who, by these laws
    You learn of, still shines on,
As pleasing-pure as erst she was,
    Though you think she lies yon,
        Graved, glow all gone.

XII

"Here are those others you used to prize.—
        But why go further we?
The Future?—Well, I would advise
        You let the future be,
            Unshown by me!

XIII

" 'Twould harrow you to see undraped
        The scenes in ripe array
That wait your globe—all worked and
            shaped;
        And I'll not, as I say,
            Bare them to-day.

XIV

"In fine, Time is a mock,—yea, such!—
        As he might well confess:
Yet hath he been believed in much,
        Though lately, under stress
            Of science, less.

XV

"And hence, of her you asked about
        At your first speaking: she
Hath, I assure you, not passed out
        Of continuity,
            But is in me.

XVI

"So thus doth Being's length transcend
    Time's ancient regal claim
To see all lengths begin and end.
    'The Fourth Dimension' fame
      Bruits as its name."

New Year's Eve, 1922.

"SO, TIME"

(The same thought resumed)

So, Time,
        Royal, sublime;
Heretofore held to be
Master and enemy,
Thief of my Love's adornings,
Despoiling her to scornings:—
The sound philosopher
Now sets him to aver
        You are nought
        But a thought
Without reality.

        Young, old
        Passioned, cold,
All the loved-lost thus
Are beings continuous,
In dateless dure abiding,
Over the present striding
With placid permanence
That knows not transience:
        Firm in the Vast,
        First, last;
Afar, yet close to us.

120

AN INQUIRY

A PHANTASY

Circumdederunt me dolores mortis.—Ps. xviii.

I SAID to It: "We grasp not what you
meant,
(Dwelling down here, so narrowly
pinched and pent)
By crowning Death the King of the Firma-
ment:
—The query I admit to be
One of unwonted size,
But it is put you sorrowingly,
And not in idle-wise."

"Sooth, since you ask me gravely," It
replied,
"Though too incisive questions I have
decried,
This shows some thought, and may be
justified.
I'll gauge its value as I go
Across the Universe,
And bear me back in a moment or so
And say, for better or worse."

121

Many years later, when It came again,
"That   matter   an   instant   back   which
    brought you pain,"
It said, "and you besought me to explain:
        Well, my forethoughtless modes to
            you
        May seem a shameless thing,
        But—I'd no meaning, that I knew,
        In crowning Death as King!"

THE FAITHFUL SWALLOW

WHEN summer shone
        Its sweetest on
An August day,
"Here evermore,"
I said, "I'll stay;
Not go away
To another shore
As fickle they!"

December came:
'Twas not the same!
I did not know
Fidelity
Would serve me so.
Frost, hunger, snow;
And now, ah me,
Too late to go!

IN SHERBORNE ABBEY

(17—)

THE moon has passed to the panes
    of the south-aisle wall,
And brought the mullioned shades and
    shines to fall
On the cheeks of a woman and man in
    a pew there, pressed
Together as they pant, and recline for
    rest.

Forms round them loom, recumbent like
    their own,
Yet differing; for they are chiselled in
    frigid stone;
In doublets are some; some mailed, as
    whilom ahorse they leapt;
And stately husbands and wives, side by
    side as they anciently slept.

124

"We are not like those," she murmurs.
    "For ever here set!"
"True, Love," he replies.   "We two are
    not marble yet."
    "And, worse," said she; "not husband
    and wife!"
    "But we soon shall be" (from him)
    "if we've life!"
A silence.   A trotting of horses is heard
    without.
The lovers scarce breathe till its echo has
    quite died out.

    "It was they!   They have passed, any-
    how!"
    "Our horse, slily hid by the conduit,
    They've missed, or they'd rushed to
    impound it!"
    "And they'll not discover us now."
    "Will not, until 'tis too late,
    And we can outface them straight!"

"Why did you make me ride in your front?"
    says she.
"To outwit the law.   That was my
    strategy.
    As I was borne off on the pillion behind
    you,
    Th'abductor was you, Dearest, let me
    remind you;

And seizure of me by an heiress is no
    felony,
Whatever to do it with me as the seizer
    may be."

Another silence falls.   And a cloud comes
    over the moon:
The print of the panes upon them en-
    feebles, as fallen in a swoon,
    Until they are left in darkness unbroke
    and profound,
As likewise are left their chill and chiselled
    neighbours around.

A Family tradition.

THE PAIR HE SAW PASS

O SAD man, now a long dead man,
　　To whom it was so real,
I picture, as 'twere yesterday,
　　How you would tell the tale!

Just wived were you, you sad dead man,
　　And "settling down," you'd say,
And had rigged the house you had reared
　　　for yourself
　　And the mate now yours alway.

You had eyed and tried each door and lock,
　　And cupboard, and bell, and glass,
When you glanced across to the road
　　　without,
　　And saw a carriage pass.

It bowled along from the old town-gate;
　　Two forms its freight, and those
Were a just-joined pair, as you discerned
　　By the favours and the bows.

And one of the pair you saw was a Fair
  Whom you had wooed awhile,
And the other you saw, with a creeping
    awe,
  Was yourself, in bridegroom style.

"And there we rode as man and wife
  In the broad blaze of the sun,"
Would you aver; yea, you with her
  You had left for another one.

"The morning," you said, my friend long
    dead,
  "Was ordinary and fine;
And yet there gleamed, it somehow
    seemed,
  At moments, a strange shine."

You hailed a boy from your garden-plot,
  And sent him along the way
To the parish church; whence word was
    brought
  No marriage had been that day.

You mused, you said; till you heard anon
  That at that hour she died
Whom once, instead of your living wife,
  You had meant to make your bride. . . .

You, dead man, dwelt in your new-built
    house
  With no great spirit or will,
And after your soon decease your spouse
  Re-mated: she lives there still.

Which should be blamed, if either can,
  The teller does not know
For your mismatch, O weird-wed man,
  Or what you thought was so.

From an old draft.

THE MOCK WIFE

IT'S a dark drama, this, and yet I know
    the house, and date;
That is to say, the where and when John
    Channing met his fate.
The house was one in High Street, seen of
    burghers still alive.
The year was some two centuries bygone;
    seventeen-hundred and five.

And dying was Channing the grocer. All
    the clocks had struck eleven,
And the watchers saw that ere the dawn his
    soul would be in Heaven;
When he said on a sudden: "I should *like*
    to kiss her before I go,—
For one last time!" They looked at each
    other and murmured, "Even so."

She'd just been haled to prison, his wife;
    yea, charged with shaping his death:
By poison, 'twas told; and now he was
    nearing the moment of his last breath:

He, witless that his young housemate was
    suspect of such a crime,
Lay thinking that his pangs were but a
    malady of the time.

Outside the room they pondered gloomily,
    wondering what to do,
As still he craved her kiss—the dying man
    who nothing knew:
"Guilty she may not be," they said; "so
    why should we torture him
In these his last few minutes of life? Yet
    how indulge his whim?"

And as he begged there piteously for what
    could not be done,
And the murder-charge had flown about the
    town to every one,
The friends around him in their trouble
    thought of a hasty plan,
And straightway set about it. Let denounce
    them all who can.

"O will you do a kindly deed—it may be
    a soul to save;
At least, great misery to a man with one
    foot in the grave?"
Thus they to the buxom woman not unlike
    his prisoned wife;
"The difference he's past seeing; it will
    soothe his sinking life."

Well, the friendly neighbour did it; and he
      kissed her; held her fast;
Kissed her again and yet again. "I—knew
      she'd—come at last!—
Where have you been?—Ah, kept away!
      —I'm sorry—overtried—
God bless you!" And he loosed her, fell
      back tiredly, and died.

His wife stood six months after on the
      scaffold before the crowd,
Ten thousand of them gathered there; fixed,
      silent, and hard-browed,
To see her strangled and burnt to dust, as
      was the verdict then
On women truly judged, or false, of doing
      to death their men.

Some of them said as they watched her
      burn: "I am glad he never knew,
Since a few hold her as innocent—think
      such she could not do!
Glad, too, that (as they tell) he thought
      she kissed him ere he died."
And they seemed to make no question that
      the cheat was justified.

THE FIGHT ON DURNOVER
MOOR

(183-)

WE'D loved, we two, some
while,
And that had come which comes when men
too much beguile;
And without more ado
My lady said: "O shame! Get home, and
hide!" But he was true.

Yes: he was true to me,
And helped me some miles homealong; and
vowing to come
Before the weeks were three,
And do in church a deed should strike all
scandal dumb.

And when we had traipsed to Grey's
great Bridge, and pitched my box
On its cope, to breathe us there,
He cried: "What wrangle's that in yonder
moor? Those knocks,
Gad, seem not to be fair!

"And a woman on her knees! . . . I'll
      go. . . . There's surely some-
      thing wrong!"
    I said: "You are tired and spent
With carrying my heavy things so far and
      long!"
    But he would go, and went.

And there I stood, steadying my box, and
      screened from none,
    Upon the crown of the bridge,
Ashamed o' my shape, as lower and lower
      slipped the sun
    Down behind Pummery Ridge. . . .

    "O you may long wait so!
Your   young   man's   done—aye,   dead!"
      they by and by ran and cried.
    "You shouldn't have let him go
And join that whorage, but have kept him
      at your side!

    "It was another wench,
Biggening as you, that he championed:
      yes, he came on straight
      With a warmth no words could
      quench
For her helpless face, as soon as ever he
      eyed her state,

"And fought her fancy-lad, who had used
         her far from well,
     So soon to make her moan,
Aye, closed with him in fight, till at a blow
         yours fell,
     His skull against a stone.

"She'd followed him there, this man who'd
         won her, and overwon,
     So, when he set to twit her
Yours couldn't abide him—him all other
         fighters shun,
     For he's a practised hitter.

"Your man moved not, and the constables
         came for the other; so he,
     He'll never make her his wife
Any more than yours will you; for they
         say that at least 'twill be
     Across the water for life."

         "O what has she brought about!"
I groaned: "this woman met here in my
         selfsame plight;
She's put another yielding heart's poor
         candle out
     By dogging her man to-night!

"He might never have done her
    his due
Of amends! But mine had bidden the
    banns for marrying me!
Why did we rest on this bridge; why rush
    to a quarrel did he
    With which he had nothing to do!"

But vain were bursts of blame:
We twain stood like and like, though
    strangers till that hour,
Foredoomed to tread our paths beneath like
    gaze and glower,
    Bear a like blushful name.

Almost the selfsame day
It fell that her time and mine came on,—
    a lad and a lass:
The father o' mine was where the worms
    waggle under the grass,
    Of hers, at Botany Bay.

LAST LOOK ROUND
ST. MARTIN'S FAIR

THE sun is like an open furnace
door,
Whose round revealed retort contains
the roar
Of fires beyond terrene;
The moon presents the lustre-lacking
face
Of a brass dial gone green,
Whose hours no eye can trace.
The unsold heathcroppers are driven
home
To the shades of the Great Forest
whence they come
By men with long cord-waistcoats in brown
monochrome.
The stars break out, and flicker in the
breeze,
It seems, that twitches the trees.—
From its hot idol soon
The fickle unresting earth has turned to a
fresh patroon—
The cold, now brighter, moon.

The woman in red, at the nut-stall
with the gun,
Lights up, and still goes on:
She's redder in the flare-lamp than
the sun
Showed it ere it was gone.
Her hands are black with loading all
the day,
And yet she treats her labour as 'twere
play,
Tosses her ear-rings, and talks ribaldry
To the young men around as natural gaiety,
And not a weary work she'd readily
stay,
And never again nut-shooting see,
Though crying, "Fire away!"

THE CARICATURE

OF the Lady Lu there were stories told,
　　For she was a woman of comely
　　　　mould,
　　In heart-experience old.

Too many a man for her whimful sake
Had borne with patience chill and ache,
　　And nightly lain awake!

This epicure in pangs, in her tooth
For more of the sweet, with a calm unruth
　　Cast eyes on a painter-youth.

Her junior he; and the bait of bliss
Which she knew to throw—not he to
　　　　miss—
　　She threw, till he dreamed her his.

To her arts not blind, he yet sued long,
As a songster jailed by a deed of wrong
　　Will shower the doer with song;

Till tried by tones now smart, now suave,
He would flee in ire, to return a slave
    Who willingly forgave.

When no! One day he left her door,
"I'll ease mine agony!" he swore,
    "And bear this thing no more!

"I'll practise a plan!" Thereon he took
Her portrait from his sketching-book,
    And, though his pencil shook,

He moulded on the real its mock;
Of beauteous brow, lip, eye, and lock
    Composed a laughingstock.

Amazed at this satire of his long lure,
Whenever he scanned it he'd scarce endure
    His laughter. 'Twas his cure.

And, even when he woke in the night,
And chanced to think of the comic sight,
    He laughed till exhausted quite.

"Why do you laugh?" she said one day
As he gazed at her in a curious way.
    "Oh—for nothing," said he. "Mere
      play."

—A gulf of years then severed the twain;
Till he heard—a painter of high attain—
     She was dying on her domain.

"And," dryly added the friend who told,
"You may know or not that, in semblance
          cold,
     She loved once, loved whole-souled;

"And that you were the man? Did you
          break your vow?
Well, well; she is good as gone by now . . .
     But you hit her, all allow!"

Ah, the blow past bearing that he received!
In his bachelor quiet he grieved and grieved;
     How cruel; how self-deceived!

Did she ever know?. . . Men pitied his
          state
As the curse of his own contrivance ate
     Like canker into his fate.

For ever that thing of his evil craft
Uprose on his grief—his mocking draught—
     Till, racked, he insanely laughed.

Thence onward folk would muse in doubt
What gloomed him so as he walked about,
     But few, or none, found out.

A LEADER OF FASHION

NEVER has she known
    The way a robin will skip and
      come,
With an eye half bold, half timorsome,
To the table's edge for a breakfast crumb:

    Nor has she seen
A streak of roseate gently drawn
Across the east, that means the dawn,
When, up and out, she foots it on:

    Nor has she heard
The rustle of the sparrow's tread
To roost in roof-holes near her head
When dusk bids her, too, seek her bed:

    Nor has she watched
Amid a stormy eve's turmoil
The pipkin slowly come to boil,
In readiness for one at toil:

Nor has she hearkened
Through the long night-time, lone and
        numb,
For sounds of sent-for help to come
Ere the swift-sinking life succumb:

Nor has she ever
Held the loved-lost one on her arm,
Attired with care his straightened form,
As if he were alive and warm:

Yea, never has she
Known, seen, heard, felt, such things as
        these,
Haps of so many in their degrees
Throughout their count of calvaries!

MIDNIGHT ON BEECHEN, 187–

ON Beechen Cliff self-commune I
    This night of mid-June, mute and
      dry;
When darkness never rises higher
Than Bath's dim concave, towers, and spire,
Last eveglow loitering in the sky

To feel the dawn, close lurking by,
The while the lamps as glow-worms lie
In a glade, myself their lonely eyer
          On Beechen Cliff:

The city sleeps below. I sigh,
For there dwells one, all testify,
To match the maddest dream's desire:
What swain with her would not aspire
To walk the world, yea, sit but nigh
          On Beechen Cliff!

THE AËROLITE

I THOUGHT a germ of Consciousness
  Escaped on an aërolite
    Aions ago
From some far globe, where no distress
Had means to mar supreme delight;

But only things abode that made
The power to feel a gift uncloyed
    Of gladsome glow,
And life unendingly displayed
Emotions loved, desired, enjoyed.

And that this stray, exotic germ
Fell wanderingly upon our sphere,
    After its wingings,
Quickened, and showed to us the worm
That gnaws vitalities native here,

And operated to unblind
Earth's old-established innocence
    Of stains and stingings,
Which grin no griefs while not opined
But cruelly tax intelligence.

"How shall we," then the seers said,
"Oust this awareness, this disease
        Called sense, here sown,
Though good, no doubt, where it was bred,
And wherein all things work to please?"

Others cried: "Nay, we rather would,
Since this untoward gift is sent
        For ends unknown,
Limit its registerings to good,
And hide from it all anguishment."

I left them pondering.   This was how
(Or so I dreamed) was waked on earth
        The mortal moan
Begot of sentience.   Maybe now
Normal unawareness waits rebirth.

THE PROSPECT

THE twigs of the birch imprint the
      December sky
  Like branching veins upon a thin old
      hand;
I think of summer-time, yes, of last July,
  When she was beneath them, greeting a
      gathered band
    Of the urban and bland.

Iced airs wheeze through the skeletoned
      hedge from the north,
  With steady snores, and a numbing that
      threatens snow,
And skaters pass; and merry boys go
      forth
  To look for slides. But well, well do I
      know
    Whither I would go!

December 1912.

147

GENITRIX LAESA

(MEASURE OF A SARUM SEQUENCE)

NATURE, through these generations
  You have nursed us with a patience
Cruelly crossed by malversations,
  Marring mother-ministry
To your multitudes, so blended
By your processes, long-tended,
And the painstaking expended
  On their chording tunefully.

But this stuff of slowest moulding,
In your fancy ever enfolding
Life that rhythmic chime is holding:
  (Yes; so deem it you, Ladye—
This "concordia discors"!)—truly,
Rather, as if some imp unruly
Twitched your artist-arm when newly
  Shaping forth your scenery!

148

Aye.　Yet seem you not to know it.
Hence your world-work needs must show it
Good in dream, in deed below it:
　　(Lady, yes: so sight it we!)
Thus, then, go on fondly thinking:
Why should man your purblind blinking
Crave to cure, when all is sinking
　　To dissolubility.

THE FADING ROSE

I SAW a rose, in bloom, but sad,
   Shedding the petals that still it had,
And I heard it say: "O where is she
Who used to come and muse on me?

"The pruner says she comes no more
Because she loves another flower,
The weeder says she's tired of me
Because I droop so suddenly.

"Because of a sweetheart she comes not,
Declares the man with the watering-pot;
'She does not come,' says he with the rake,
'Because all women are fickle in make.'

"He with the spade and humorous leer
Says: 'Know, I delve elsewhere than here,
Mid text-writ stones and grassy heaps,
Round which a curious silence creeps.

" 'She must get to you underground
If any way at all be found,
For, clad in her beauty, marble's kin,
'Tis there I have laid her and trod her
      in.' "

WHEN OATS WERE REAPED

THAT day when oats were reaped, and
    wheat was ripe, and barley ripening,
The road-dust hot, and the bleaching
    grasses dry,
I walked along and said,
While looking just ahead to where some
    silent people lie:

"I wounded one who's there, and now
    know well I wounded her;
    But, ah, she does not know that she
    wounded me!"
And not an air stirred,
Nor a bill of any bird; and no response
    accorded she.

August 1913.

152

LOUIE

I AM forgetting Louie the buoyant;
　　Why not raise her phantom, too,
　　　　Here in daylight
　　　　With the elect one's?
She will never thrust the foremost figure
　　　　out of view!

　　Mid this heat, in gauzy muslin
　　See I Louie's life-lit brow
　　　　Here in daylight
　　　　By the elect one's.—
Long two strangers they and far apart;
　　　　such neighbours now!

July 1913.

153

"SHE OPENED THE DOOR"

SHE opened the door of the West to me,
    With its loud sea-lashings,
    And cliff-side clashings
Of waters rife with revelry.

She opened the door of Romance to me,
    The door from a cell
    I had known too well,
Too long, till then, and was fain to flee.

She opened the door of a Love to me,
    That passed the wry
    World-welters by
As far as the arching blue the lea.

She opens the door of the Past to me,
    Its magic lights,
    Its heavenly heights,
When forward little is to see!

  1913.

"WHAT'S THERE TO TELL?"

(SONG)

WHAT'S there to tell of the world
    More than is told?
—Into its vortex hurled,
    Out of it rolled,
Can we yet more of the world
    Find to be told?
        Lalla-la, lu!

If some could last alive
    Much might be told;
Yes, gladness might survive;
    But they go cold—
Each and each late alive—
    All their tale told.
        Lalla-la, lu!

There's little more of the world,
    Then, to be told;

Had ever life unfurled
    Joys manifold
There had been more of the world
    Left to be told.
        Lalla-la, lalla-la, lalla-la, lu!

190—.

THE HARBOUR BRIDGE

FROM here, the quay, one looks above
    to mark
The bridge across the harbour, hanging
    dark
Against the day's-end sky, fair-green in
    glow
Over and under the middle archway's bow:
It draws its skeleton where the sun has set,
Yea, clear from cutwater to parapet;
On which mild glow, too, lines of rope and
    spar
    Trace themselves black as char.

Down here in shade we hear the painters
    shift
Against the bollards with a drowsy lift,
As moved by the incoming stealthy tide.
High up across the bridge the burghers
    glide
As cut black-paper portraits hastening on
In conversation none knows what upon:
Their sharp-edged lips move quickly word
    by word
    To speech that is not heard.

There trails the dreamful girl, who leans
     and stops,
There presses the practical woman to the
     shops,
There is a sailor, meeting his wife with a
     start,
And we, drawn nearer, judge they are
     keeping apart.
Both pause. She says: "I've looked for
     you. I thought
We'd make it up." Then no words can
     be caught.
At last: "Won't you come home?" She
     moves still nigher:
    " 'Tis comfortable, with a fire."

"No," he says gloomily. "And, anyhow,
I can't give up the other woman now:
You should have talked like that in former
     days,
When I was last home." They go differ-
     ent ways.
And the west dims, and yellow lamplights
     shine:
And soon above, like lamps more opaline,
White stars ghost forth, that care not for
     men's wives,
    Or any other lives.

Weymouth.

VAGRANT'S SONG

(WITH AN OLD WESSEX REFRAIN)

I

WHEN a dark-eyed dawn
    Crawls forth, cloud-drawn,
And starlings doubt the night-time's close;
    And "three months yet,"
    They seem to fret,
"Before we cease us slaves of snows,
    And sun returns
    To loose the burns,
And this wild woe called Winter goes!"—
    O a hollow tree
    Is as good for me
As a house where the back-brand glows!
Che-hane, mother; che-hane, mother,
    As a house where the back-brand glows!

Line 12: "back-brand"—the log which used to be
laid at the back of a wood fire.

II

When autumn brings
A whirr of wings
Among the evergreens around,
And sundry thrills
About their quills
Awe rooks, and misgivings abound,
And the joyless pines
In leaning lines
Protect from gales the lower ground,
O a hollow tree
Is as good for me
As a house of a thousand pound!
Che-hane, mother; che-hane, mother,
As a house of a thousand pound!

FARMER DUNMAN'S FUNERAL

"BURY me on a Sunday,"
　　He said; "so as to see
Poor folk there.   'Tis their one day
　　To spare for following me."

And mindful of that Sunday,
　　He wrote, while he was well,
On ten rum-bottles one day,
　　"Drink for my funeral."

They buried him on a Sunday,
　　That folk should not be balked
His wish, as 'twas their one day:
　　And forty couple walked.

They said: "To have it Sunday
　　Was always his concern;
His meaning being that one day
　　He'd do us a good turn.

161

"We must, had it been Monday,
 Have got it over soon,
But now we gain, being Sunday,
 A jolly afternoon."

THE SEXTON AT LONGPUDDLE

HE passes down the churchyard track
　　On his way to toll the bell;
And stops, and looks at the graves around,
And notes each finished and greening
　　mound
　　　　Complacently,
　　　　As their shaper he,
　　And one who can do it well.
And, with a prosperous sense of his doing,
　　　　Thinks he'll not lack
Plenty such work in the long ensuing
　　　　Futurity.
　　　　For people will always die,
　　　　And he will always be nigh
　　　　　To shape their cell.

THE HARVEST-SUPPER

(*Circa* 1850)

NELL and the other maids danced their
best
  With the Scotch Greys in the barn;
These had been asked to the harvest-
feast;
  Red shapes amid the corn.

Nell and the other maids sat in a row
  Within the benched barn-nook;
Nell led the songs of long ago
  She'd learnt from never a book.

She sang of the false Sir John of old,
  The lover who witched to win,
And the parrot, and cage of glittering gold;
  And the other maids joined in.

Then whispered to her a gallant Grey,
  "Dear, sing that ballet again!
For a bonnier mouth in a bonnier way
  Has sung not anywhen!"

As she loosed her lips anew there sighed
  To Nell through the dark barn-door
The voice of her Love from the night
    outside,
  Who was buried the month before:

"O Nell, can you sing ballets there,
  And I out here in the clay,
Of lovers false of yore, nor care
  What you vowed to me one day!

"O can you dance with soldiers bold,
  Who kiss when dancing's done,
Your little waist within their hold,
  As ancient troth were none!"

She cried: "My heart is pierced with a
    wound!
  There's something outside the wall
That calls me forth to a greening mound:
  I can sing no more at all!

"My old Love rises from the worms,
  Just as he used to be,
And I must let gay gallants' arms
  No more encircle me!"

They bore her home from the merry-
    making;
Bad dreams disturbed her bed:
"Nevermore will I dance and sing,"
    Mourned Nell; "and never wed!"

AT A PAUSE IN A COUNTRY DANCE

(MIDDLE OF LAST CENTURY)

THEY stood at the foot of the figure,
    And panted: they'd danced it down
        through—
That "Dashing White Serjeant" they loved
        so:—
A window, uncurtained, was nigh them
That end of the room.   Thence in view

Outside it a valley updrew,
Where the frozen moon lit frozen snow:
At the furthermost reach of the valley
A light from a window shone low.
"They are inside that window," said she,

As she looked.   "They sit up there for me;
And baby is sleeping there, too."
He glanced.   "Yes," he said.   "Never
        mind,"
Let's foot our way up again; do!
And dance down the line as before.

"What's the world to us, meeting once
        more!"
"—Not much, when your husband full
        trusts you,
And thinks the child his that I bore!"
He was silent.   The fiddlers six-eighted
With even more passionate vigour.

The pair swept again up the figure,
The child's cuckoo-father and she,
And the next couples threaded below,
And the twain wove their way to the top
Of "The Dashing White Serjeant" they
        loved so,
Restarting: right, left, to and fro.

—From the homestead, seen yon, the small
        glow
Still adventured forth over the white,
Where the child slept, unknowing who
        sired it,
In the cradle of wicker tucked tight,
And its grandparents, nodding, admired it
In elbow-chairs through the slow night.

ON THE PORTRAIT OF A WOMAN
ABOUT TO BE HANGED

COMELY and capable one of our race,
 Posing there in your gown of grace,
 Plain, yet becoming;
   Could subtlest breast
   Ever have guessed
What was behind that innocent face,
  Drumming, drumming!

Would that your Causer, ere knoll your
   knell
For this riot of passion, might deign to tell
  Why, since It made you
   Sound in the germ,
   It sent a worm
To madden Its handiwork, when It might
   well
  Not have assayed you,

Not have implanted, to your deep rue,
The Clytaemnestra spirit in you,

And with purblind vision
Sowed a tare
In a field so fair,
And a thing of symmetry, seemly to view,
Brought to derision!

January 6, 1923.

THE CHURCH AND THE WEDDING

"I'LL restore this old church for our
      marriage:
   I've ordered the plans:
Style of wedding your choice—foot or
      carriage—
   By licence, or banns."

He restored it, as though built newly:
   The bishop was won
To preach, who pronounced it truly
   A thing well done.

But the wedding waits; long, long has
      waited;
   And guesswork is dumb
Why those who were there to have mated
   Do not come.

And when the nights moan like the wailings
    Of souls sore-tried,
The folk say who pass the church-palings
    They hear inside

Strange sounds as of anger and sadness
    That cut the heart's core,
And shaken words bitter to madness;
    And then no more.

THE SHIVER

FIVE long clangs from the house-clock
    nigh,
        And I woke with a sigh:
Stars wore west like a slow tide flowing,
And my lover had told yesternight of his
    going,—
That at this gray hour he'd be hasting by,

Starting betimes on a journey afar:—
        So, casement ajar,
I eyed in the upland pasture his figure,
A dim dumb speck, growing darker and
    bigger,
Then smalling to nought where the nut-
    trees are.

He could not bend his track to my window,
    he'd said,
        Being hurried ahead:
But I wished he had tried to!—and then
    felt a shiver,

Corpse-cold, as he sank toward the town
    by the river;
And back I went sadly and slowly to bed.

What meant my shiver while seeing him
    pass
        As a dot on the grass
I surmised not then. But later I knew it
When came again he; and my words out-
    drew it,
As said he: "It's hard for your bearing,
    alas!

"But I've seen, I have clasped, where the
    smart ships plough,
        One of far brighter brow.
A sea-goddess.   Shiver not.   One far
    rarer
In gifts than I find thee; yea, warmer and
    fairer:—
I seek her again; and I love you not now."

"NOT ONLY I"

N OT only I
      Am doomed awhile to lie
In this close bin with earthen sides;
But the things I thought, and the songs I
    sang,
And the hopes I had, and the passioned
        pang
      For people I knew
      Who passed before me,
  Whose memory barely abides;
      And the visions I drew
      That daily upbore me!

  And the joyous springs and summers,
  And the jaunts with blithe new-
    comers,
And my plans and appearances; drives
  and rides
That fanned my face to a lively red;
      And the grays and blues
      Of the far-off views,

That nobody else discerned outspread;
And little achievements for blame or
      praise;
Things left undone; things left unsaid;
            In brief, my days!

Compressed here in six feet by two,
            In secrecy
            To lie with me
            Till the Call shall be,
Are all these things I knew,
Which cannot be handed on;
Strange happenings quite unrecorded,
Lost to the world and disregarded,
That only thinks: "Here moulders till
      Doom's-dawn
      A woman's skeleton."

SHE SAW HIM, SHE SAID

"WHY, I saw you with the sexton,
        outside the church-door,
So I did not hurry me home,
Thinking you'd not be come,
Having something to him to say —
Yes; 'twas you, Dear, though you seemed
        sad, heart-sore;
How fast you've got therefrom!"

"I've not been out. I've watched the
        moon through the birch,
And heard the bell toll. Yes,
Like a passing soul in distress!"
"—But no bell's tolled to-day?" . . .
His face looked strange, like the face of
        him seen by the church,
And she sank to musefulness.

ONCE AT SWANAGE

THE spray sprang up across the cusps
    of the moon,
      And all its light loomed green
      As a witch-flame's weirdsome sheen
At the minute of an incantation scene;
And it greened our gaze—that night at
    demilune.

Roaring high and roaring low was the sea
      Behind the headland shores:
      It symboled the slamming of doors,
Or a regiment hurrying over hollow
    floors. . . .
And there we two stood, hands clasped;
      I and she!

THE FLOWER'S TRAGEDY

IN the bedchamber window, near the
    glass,
Stood the little flower in the little vase,
        Unnoticed quite
        For a whole fortnight,
And withered for lack of watering
To a skeleton mere—a mummied thing.

But it was not much, mid a world of
    teen,
That a flower should waste in a nook
    unseen!

One needed no thought to ascertain
How it happened; that when she went in
        the rain
        To return here not,
        She was mindless what
She had left here to perish.—Ah, well:
    for an hour
I wished I had not found the flower!

Yet it was not much. And she never had
    known
Of the flower's fate; nor it of her own.

AT THE AQUATIC SPORTS

WITH their backs to the sea two
      fiddlers stand
Facing the concourse on the strand,
    And a third man who sings.
The sports proceed; there are crab-
      catchings;
The people laugh as levity spreads,
Yet these three do not turn their heads
    To see whence the merriment springs.

They cease their music, but even then
They stand as before, do those three men,
    Though pausing, nought to do:
They never face to the seaward view
To enjoy the contests, add their cheer,
So wholly is their being here
    A business they pursue.

A WATCHER'S REGRET

J. E.'S STORY

I SLEPT across the front of the clock,
   Close to the long case-door;
The hours were brought by their brazen
    knock
   To my ear as the slow nights wore.

Thus did I, she being sick to death,
   That each hour as it belled
Should wake me to rise, and learn by her
    breath
   Whether her strength still held.

Yet though throughout life's midnights all
   I would have watched till spent
For her dear sake, I missed the call
   Of the hour in which she went.

HORSES ABOARD

HORSES in horsecloths stand in a row
On board the huge ship, that at
last lets go:
Whither are they sailing? They do not
know,
Nor what for, nor how.——
They are horses of war,
And are going to where there is fighting
afar;
But they gaze through their eye-holes un-
witting they are,
And that in some wilderness, gaunt and
ghast,
Their bones will bleach ere a year has
passed,
And the item be as "war-waste" classed.——
And when the band booms, and the folk
say "Good-bye!"
And the shore slides astern, they appear
wrenched awry
From the scheme Nature planned for them,
——wondering why.

THE HISTORY OF AN HOUR

VAIN is the wish to try rhyming it,
    writing it!
Pen cannot weld into words what it was;
Time will be squandered in toil at in-
    diting it;
        Clear is the cause!

Yea, 'twas too satiate with soul, too
    ethereal;
June-morning scents of a rose-bush in
    flower
Catch in a clap-net of hempen material;
        So catch that hour!

THE MISSED TRAIN

HOW I was caught
     Hieing home, after days of
          allure,
And forced to an inn—small, obscure—
     At the junction, gloom-fraught.

     How civil my face
To get them to chamber me there—
A roof I had scorned, scarce aware
     That it stood at the place.

     And how all the night
I had dreams of the unwitting cause
Of my lodgment. How lonely I was;
     How consoled by her sprite!

     Thus onetime to me . . .
Dim wastes of dead years bar away
Then from now. But such happenings
          to-day
     Fall to lovers, may be!

Years, years as shoaled seas,
Truly, stretch now between!   Less and
    less
Shrink the visions then vast in me.—Yes,
    Then in me: Now in these.

UNDER HIGH-STOY HILL

FOUR climbed High-Stoy from Ivel-
        wards,
Where hedge meets hedge, and cart-ruts
        wind,
        Chattering like birds,
And knowing not what lay behind.

We laughed beneath the moonlight blink,
Said supper would be to our mind,
        And did not think
Of Time, and what might lie behind. . . .

The moon still meets that tree-tipped
        height,
The road—as then—still trails inclined;
        But since that night
We have well learnt what lay behind!

For all of the four then climbing here
But one are ghosts, and he brow-lined;
        With him they fare,
Yet speak not of what lies behind.

AT THE MILL

O MILLER KNOX, whom we knew
    well,
  And the mill, and the floury flours,
And the corn,— and those two women,
    And infants—yours!

The sun was shining when you rode
  To market on that day:
The sun was set when home-along
  You ambled in the gray,
And gathered what had taken place
    While you were away.

O Miller Knox, 'twas grief to see
  Your good wife hanging there
By her own rash and passionate hand,
    In a throe of despair;

And those two children, one by her,
  And one by the waiting-maid,
Borne the same hour, and you afar,
    And she past aid.

And though sometimes you walk of nights,
  Sleepless, to Yalbury Brow,
And glance the graveyard way, and grunt,
  " 'Twas not much, anyhow:
She shouldn't ha' minded!" nought it
    helps
      To say that now.

And the water dribbles down your wheel,
  Your mead blooms green and gold,
And birds twit in your apple-boughs
      Just as of old,

ALIKE AND UNLIKE

(GREAT-ORME'S HEAD)

WE watched the selfsame scene on
    that long drive,
Saw the magnificent purples, as one eye,
Of those near mountains; saw the storm
    arrive;
Laid up the sight in memory, you and I,
As if for joint recallings by and by.

But our eye-records, like in hue and line,
Had superimposed on them, that very day,
Gravings on your side deep, but slight on
    mine!—
Tending to sever us thenceforth alway;
Mine commonplace; yours tragic, grue-
    some, gray.

THE THING UNPLANNED

THE white winter sun struck its stroke
    on the bridge,
    The meadow-rills rippled and gleamed
As I left the thatched post-office, just by
    the ridge,
And dropped in my pocket her long tender
    letter,
With: "This must be snapped! it is more
    than it seemed;
    And now is the opportune time!"

But against what I willed worked the
    surging sublime
    Of the thing that I did—the thing
    better!

THE SHEEP BOY

A YAWNING, sullied concave
    Of purple, spread as an ocean
        wave
Entroughed on a morning of swell
    and sway
After a night when wind-fiends have been
    heard to rave:
Thus was the Heath called "Draäts",
    on an August day.

Suddenly there intunes a hum:
This side, that side, it seems to come.
From the purple in myriads rise the
    bees
With consternation mid their rapt
    employ.
So headstrongly each speeds him
    past, and flees,
    As to strike the face of the shepherd-
      boy.

Awhile he waits, and wonders what
    they mean;
Till none is left upon the shagged
    demesne.

To learn what ails, the sheep-boy
    looks around;
    Behind him, out of the sea in swirls
Flexuous and solid, clammy vapour-curls
Are rolling over Pokeswell Hills to the
    inland ground.
Into the heath they sail,
And travel up the vale
Like the moving pillar of cloud raised by
    the Israelite:—
In a trice the lonely sheep-boy seen so late
    ago,
        Draäts'-Hollow in gorgeous blow,
        And Kite-Hill's regal glow,
Are viewless—folded into those creeping
    scrolls of white.

On Rainbarrows.

RETTY'S PHASES

I

RETTY used to shake her head,
    Look with wicked eye;
Say, "I'd tease you, simplehead,
    If I cared to try!"
Then she'd hot-up scarlet red,
    Stilly step away,
Much afraid that what she'd said
    Sounded bold to say.

II

Retty used to think she loved
    (Just a little) me
Not untruly, as it proved
    Afterwards to be.
For, when weakness forced her rest
    If we walked a mile,
She would whisper she was blest
    By my clasp awhile.

III

Retty used at last to say
  When she neared the Vale,
"Mind that you, Dear, on that day
  Ring my wedding peal!"
And we all, with pulsing pride,
  Vigorous sounding gave
Those six bells, the while outside
  John filled in her grave.

IV

Retty used to draw me down
  To the turfy heaps,
Where, with yeoman, squire, and clown
  Noticeless she sleeps.
Now her silent slumber-place
  Seldom do I know,
For when last I saw her face
  Was so long ago!

From an old draft of 1868.

NOTE.—In many villages it was customary after the
funeral of an unmarried young woman to ring a peal as
for her wedding while the grave was being filled in, as if
Death were not to be allowed to balk her of bridal
honours. Young unmarried men were always her bearers.

A POOR MAN AND A LADY

WE knew it was not a valid thing,
    And only sanct in the sight of God
(To use your phrase), as with fervent nod
You swore your assent when I placed the
    ring
On your pale slim hand. Our whispering
Was soft as the fan of a turtledove
That round our heads might have seemed
    to wing;
So solemn were we; so sincere our love.

We could do no better; and thus it stood
Through a time of timorous secret bliss,
Till we were divided, and never a kiss
Of mine could touch you, or likelihood
Illumed our sky that we might, or should
Be each to each in the world's wide eye
What we were unviewed; and our vows
    make good
In the presence of parents and standers by.

I was a striver with deeds to do,
And little enough to do them with,
And a comely woman of noble kith,
With a courtly match to make, were you;
And we both were young; and though
    sterling-true
You had proved to our pledge under
    previous strains,
Our "union," as we called it, grew
Less grave to your eyes in your town
    campaigns.

Well: the woeful neared, you needn't be
    told:
The current news-sheets clarioned soon
That you would be wived on a summer
    noon
By a man of illustrious line and old:
Nor better nor worse than the manifold
Of marriages made, had there not been
Our faith-swearing when fervent-souled,
Which, to me, seemed a breachless bar
    between.

We met in a Mayfair church, alone:
  (The request was mine, which you yielded
    to.)
"But we were not married at all!" urged
    you:
"Why, of course we were!" I said. Your
    tone,

I noted, was world-wise. You went on:
" 'Twas sweet while it lasted. But you
    well know
That law is law. He'll be, anon,
My husband *really*. You, Dear, weren't
    so."

"I wished—but to learn if——" faltered
    I,
And stopped.   "But I'll sting you not.
    Farewell!"
And we parted.—Do you recall the hell
That tolled by chance as we said good-
    bye? . . .
I saw you no more. The track of a high,
Sweet, liberal lady you've doubtless trod.
—All's past! No heart was burst thereby,
And no one knew, unless it was God.

NOTE.—The foregoing was intended to preserve an
episode in the story of "The Poor Man and the Lady,"
written in 1868, and, like these lines, in the first person;
but never printed, and ultimately destroyed.

AN EXPOSTULATION

WHY want to go afar
      Where pitfalls are,
When all we swains adore
Your featness more and more
As heroine of our artless masquings here,
And count few Wessex' daughters half so
    dear?

Why paint your appealing face,
      When its born grace
Is such no skill can match
With powder, puff, or patch,
Whose every touch defames your bloom-
    fulness,
And with each stain increases our distress?

Yea, is it not enough
      That (rare or rough
Your lines here) all uphold you,
And as with wings enfold you,
But you must needs desert the kine-cropt
    vale
Wherein your foredames gaily filled the
    pail?

TO A SEA-CLIFF

(DURLSTON HEAD)

LEND me an ear
    While I read you here
A page from your history,
    Old cliff—not known
    To your solid stone,
Yet yours inseparably.

    Near to your crown
    There once sat down
A silent listless pair;
    And the sunset ended,
    And dark descended,
And still the twain sat there.

    Past your jutting head
    Then a line-ship sped,
Lit brightly as a city;
    And she sobbed: "There goes
    A man who knows
I am his, beyond God's pity!"

He slid apart
Who had thought her heart
His own, and not aboard
A bark, sea-bound. . . .
That night they found
Between them lay a sword.

THE ECHO ELF ANSWERS

HOW much shall I love her?
    For life, or not long?
  "Not long."

Alas! When forget her?
In years, or by June?
    "By June."

And whom woo I after?
No one, or a throng?
    "A throng."

Of these shall I wed one
Long hence, or quite soon?
    "Quite soon."

And which will my bride be?
The right or the wrong?
    "The wrong."

And my remedy—what kind?
Wealth-wove, or earth-hewn?
    "Earth-hewn."

CYNIC'S EPITAPH

A RACE with the sun as he downed
    I ran at evetide,
Intent who should first gain the ground
    And there hide.

He beat me by some minutes then,
    But I triumphed anon,
For when he'd to rise up again
    I stayed on.

A BEAUTY'S SOLILOQUY
DURING HER HONEYMOON

TOO late, too late! I did not know
    my fairness
    Would catch the world's keen eyes so!
How the men look at me! My radiant
    rareness
    I deemed not they would prize so!

That I was a peach for any man's possession
    Why did not some one say
Before I leased myself in an hour's obsession
    To this dull mate for aye!

His days are mine. I am one who cannot
    steal her
    Ahead of his plodding pace:
As he is, so am I. One doomed to feel her
    A wasted form and face!

I was so blind!   It did sometimes just strike
      me
    All girls were not as I,
But, dwelling much alone, how few were
      like me
    I could not well descry;

Till, at this Grand Hotel, all looks bend
      on me
    In homage as I pass
To take my seat at breakfast, dinner,—con
      me
    As poorly spoused, alas!

I was too young.   I dwelt too much on
      duty:
    If I had guessed my powers
Where might have sailed this cargo of choice
      beauty
    In its unanchored hours!

Well, husband, poor plain man; I've lost
      life's battle!—
    Come—let them look at me.
O damn, don't show in your looks that I'm
      your chattel
    Quite so emphatically!

In a London Hotel, 1892.

DONAGHADEE

(SONG)

I'VE never gone to Donaghadee,
    That vague far townlet by the sea;
In Donaghadee I shall never be:
Then why do I sing of Donaghadee,
That I know not in a faint degree? . . .
—Well, once a woman wrote to me
With a tender pen from Donaghadee.

"Susan," I've sung, "Pride of Kildare,"
Because I'd heard of a Susan there,
The "Irish Washerwoman's" capers
I've shared for hours to midnight tapers,
And "Kitty O'Linch" has made me spin
Till dust rose high, and day broke in:
That other "Kitty, of Coleraine,"
Too, set me aching in heart and brain:
While "Kathleen Mavourneen," of course,
    would ring
When that girl learnt to make me sing.

Then there was "Irish Molly O"
I tuned as "the fairest one I know,"
And "Nancy Dawson," if I remember,
Rhymed sweet in moonlight one September.

But the damsel who once wrote so free
And tender toned from Donaghadee,
Is a woman who has no name for me—
Moving sylph-like, mysteriously,
(For doubtless, of that sort is she)
In the pathways of her destiny;
But that is where I never shall be;—
And yet I sing of Donaghadee!

HE INADVERTENTLY CURES
HIS LOVE-PAINS

(SONG)

I SAID: "O let me sing the praise
Of her who sweetly racks my days,—
Her I adore;
Her lips, her eyes, her moods, her ways!"

In miseries of pulse and pang
I strung my harp, and straightway sang
As none before:—
To wondrous words my quavers rang!

Thus I let heartaches lilt my verse,
Which suaged and soothed, and made
disperse
The smarts I bore
To quiet like a sepulchre's.

But, eased, the days that thrilled ere then
Lost value; and I ask, O when,
And how, restore
Those old sweet agonies again!

THE PEACH PEAL

(AFTER FOUR YEARS OF SILENCE)

SAID a wistful daw in Saint Peter's
    tower,
High above Casterbridge slates and tiles,
Why do the walls of my Gothic bower
Shiver, and shrill out sounds for miles?
    This gray old rubble
    Has scorned such din
    Since I knew trouble
    And joy herein.
    How still did abide them
    These bells now swung,
    While our nest beside them
    Securely clung! . . .
    It means some snare
    For our feet or wings;
    But I'll be ware
    Of such baleful things!"
And forth he flew from his louvred niche
To take up life in a damp dark ditch.

—So mortal motives are misread,
And false designs attributed,
In upper spheres of straws and sticks,
Or lower, of pens and politics.

At the end of the War.

LADY VI

THERE goes the Lady Vi. How well,
   How well I know the spectacle
   The earth presents
   And its events
   To her sweet sight
   Each day and night!

"Life is a wheeling show, with *me*
As its pivot of interest constantly.
Below in the hollows of towns is sin,
Like a blue brimstone mist therein,
Which makes men lively who plunge amid
      it,
But wrongfully, and wives forbid it.
London is a place for prancing
Along the Row and, later, dancing
Till dawn, with tightening arm-elbow-
      ments
As hours warm up to tender moments.

Travel is piquant, and most thrilling
If, further, joined to big-game killing:
At home, too, hunting, hounds full cry,
When Reynard nears his time to die,
'Tis glee to mark his figure flag,
And how his brush begins to drag,
Till, his earth reached by many a wend,
He finds it *stopped*, and meets his end.

"Religion is good for all who are meek;
It stays in the Bible through the week,
And floats about the house on Sundays,
But does not linger on till Mondays.
The ten Commandments in one's prime
Are matter for another time,
While griefs and graves and things allied
In well-bred talk one keeps outside."

A POPULAR PERSONAGE
AT HOME

"I LIVE here: 'Wessex' is my name:
    I am a dog known rather well.
i guard the house; but how that came
To be my whim I cannot tell.

"With a leap and a heart elate I go
At the end of an hour's expectancy
To take a walk of a mile or so
With the folk I let live here with me.

"Along the path, amid the grass
I sniff, and find out rarest smells
For rolling over as I pass
The open fields towards the dells.

"No doubt I shall always cross this sill,
And turn the corner, and stand steady,
Gazing back for my mistress till
She reaches where I have run already,

"And that this meadow with its brook,
And bulrush, even as it appears
As I plunge by with hasty look,
Will stay the same a thousand years."

Thus "Wessex."   But a dubious ray
At times informs his steadfast eye,
Just for a trice, as though to say,
"Yet, will this pass, and pass shall I?"

1924.

INSCRIPTIONS FOR A PEAL
OF EIGHT BELLS

AFTER A RESTORATION

I. THOMAS TREMBLE new-
made me
Eighteen hundred and fifty-three:
Why he did I fail to see.

II. I was well-toned by William Brine,
Seventeen hundred and twenty-
nine;
Now, re-cast, I weakly whine!

III. Fifteen hundred used to be
My date, but since they melted me
'Tis only eighteen fifty-three.

IV. Henry Hopkins got me made,
And I summon folk as bade;
Not to much purpose, I'm afraid!

v. I likewise; for I bang and bid
In commoner metal than I did,
Some of me being stolen and hid.

214

VI. I, too, since in a mould they flung me,
Drained my silver, and rehung me,
So that in tin-like tones I tongue me.

VII. In nineteen hundred, so 'tis said,
They cut my canon off my head,
And made me look scalped, scraped,
and dead.

VIII. I'm the peal's tenor still, but rue it!
Once it took two to swing me
through it:
Now I'm rehung, one dolt can do it.

A REFUSAL

SAID the grave Dean of Westminster:
  Mine is the best minster
Seen in Great Britain,
As many have written,
So therefore I cannot
Rule here if I ban not
Such liberty-taking
As movements for making
Its greyness environ
The memory of Byron,
Which some are demanding
Who think them of standing,
But in my own viewing
Require some subduing
For tendering suggestions
On Abbey-wall questions
That must interfere here
With my proper sphere here,
And bring to disaster
This fane and its master,
Whose dict is but Christian
Though nicknamed Philistian.

A lax Christian charity—
No mental clarity
Ruling its movements
For fabric improvements—
Demands admonition
And strict supervision
When bent on enshrining
Rapscallions, and signing
Their names on God's stonework,
As if like His own work
Were their lucubrations:
And passed is my patience
That such a creed-scorner
(Not mentioning horner)
Should claim Poet's Corner.

'Tis urged that some sinners
Are here for worms' dinners
Already in person;
That he could not worsen
The walls by a name mere
With men of such fame here.
Yet nay; they but leaven
The others in heaven
In just true proportion,
While more mean distortion.

'Twill next be expected
That I get erected
To Shelley a tablet

In some niche or gablet.
Then—what makes my skin burn,
Yea, forehead to chin burn—
That I ensconce Swinburne!

August 1924.

EPITAPH ON A PESSIMIST

I'M Smith of Stoke, aged sixty-odd,
   I've lived without a dame
From youth-time on; and would to God
   My dad had done the same.

From the French.

THE PROTEAN MAIDEN

(SONG)

THIS single girl is two girls:
    How strange such things should be!
One noon eclipsed by few girls,
    The next no beauty she.

And daily cries the lover,
    In voice and feature vext:
"My last impression of her
    Is never to be the next!

"She's plain: I will forget her!
    She's turned to fair. Ah no,
Forget?—not I! I'll pet her
    With kisses swift and slow."

A WATERING-PLACE LADY
INVENTORIED

A SWEETNESS of temper unsurpassed
    and unforgettable,
A mole on the cheek whose absence would
    have been regrettable,
A ripple of pleasant converse full of
    modulation,
A bearing of inconveniences without vexa-
    tion,
Till a cynic would find her amiability
    provoking,
Tempting him to indulge in mean and
    wicked joking.

Flawlessly oval of face, especially cheek and
    chin,
With a glance of a quality that beckoned
    for a glance akin,
A habit of swift assent to any intelligence
    broken,
Before the fact to be conveyed was fully
    spoken

And she could know to what her colloquist
    would win her,—
This from a too alive impulsion to sym-
    pathy in her,—
All with a sense of the ridiculous, keen yet
    charitable;
In brief, a rich, profuse attractiveness
    unnarratable.

I should have added her hints that her
    husband prized her but slenderly,
And that (with a sigh) 'twas a pity she'd
    no one to treat her tenderly.

THE SEA FIGHT

31 *May*: 1916

IN MEMORIAM CAPTAIN PROWSE

DOWN went the grand "Queen
Mary,"
"Queen Mary's" captain, and her crew;
The brunt of battle bare he,
And he died;
And he died, as heroes do.

More really now we view him,
More really lives he, moves with men,
Than while on earth we knew him
As our fellow,
As our fellow-denizen.

Maybe amid the changes
Of ocean's caverned dim profound,
Gaily his spirit ranges
With his comrades
With his comrades all around.

1916.

PARADOX

(M. H.)

THOUGH out of sight now, and as
        more not the least to us;
Comes she in sorrows, as one bringing
        peace to us?
Lost to each meadow, each hill-top, each
        tree around,
Yet the whole truth may her largened
        sight see around?
      Always away from us
      She may not stray from us!
Can she, then, know how men's fatings
        befall?
Yea indeed, may know well; even know
        thereof all.

THE ROVER COME HOME

H E'S journeyed through America
  From Canso Cape to Horn,
And from East Indian Comorin
  To Behring's Strait forlorn;
He's felled trees in the backwoods,
  In swamps has gasped for breath;
In Tropic heats, in Polar ice,
  Has often prayed for death.

He has fought and bled in civil wars
  Of no concern to him,
Has shot his fellows—beasts and men—
  At risk of life and limb.
He has suffered fluxes, fevers,
  Agues, and ills allied,
And now he's home. You look at him
  As he talks by your fireside.

And what is written in his glance
  Stressed by such foreign wear,
After such alien circumstance
  What does his face declare?

His mother's; she who saw him not
  After his starting year,
Who never left her native spot,
  And lies in the churchyard near.

"KNOWN HAD I"

(SONG)

KNOWN had I what I knew not
    When we met eye to eye,
That thenceforth I should view not
    Again beneath the sky
So truefooted a farer
    As you who faced me then,
My path had been a rarer
    Than it figures among men!

I would have trod beside you
    To guard your feet all day,
And borne at night to guide you
    A lantern on your way:
Would not have left you lonely
    With wringing doubt, to cow
Old hope, if I could only
    Have known what I know now.

THE PAT OF BUTTER

ONCE, at the Agricultural Show,
　　We tasted—all so yellow—
　　Those butter-pats, cool and mellow!
Each taste I still remember, though
　　It was so long ago

This spoke of the grass of Netherhay,
　　And this of Kingcomb Hill,
　　And this of Coker Rill:
Which was the prime I could not say
　　Of all those tried that day,

Till she, the fair and wicked-eyed,
　　Held out a pat to me:
　　Then felt I all Yeo-Lea
Was by her sample sheer outvied;
　　And, "This is the best," I cried.

BAGS OF MEAT

"HERE'S a fine bag of meat,"
      Says the master-auctioneer,
As the timid, quivering steer,
Starting a couple of feet
At the prod of a drover's stick,
And trotting lightly and quick,
A ticket stuck on his rump,
Enters with a bewildered jump.

"Where he's lived lately, friends,
I'd live till lifetime ends:
They've a whole life everyday
Down there in the Vale, have they!
He'd be worth the money to kill
And give away Christmas for good-will."

"Now here's a heifer—worth more
Than bid, were she bone-poor;
Yet she's round as a barrel of beer";
"She's a plum," said the second auctioneer.

229

"Now this young bull—for thirty pound?
   Worth that to manure your ground!"
   "Or to stand," chimed the second one,
   "And have his picter done!"
The beast was rapped on the horns and
     snout
   To make him turn about.
"Well," cried a buyer, "another crown—
Since I've dragged here from Taunton
     Town!"

   "That calf, she sucked three cows,
   Which is not matched for bouse
   In the nurseries of high life
By the first-born of a nobleman's wife!"
The stick falls, meaning, "A true tale's
     told,"
On the buttock of the creature sold,
   And the buyer leans over and snips
His mark on one of the animal's hips.

   Each beast, when driven in,
Looks round at the ring of bidders there
With a much-amazed reproachful stare,
   As at unnatural kin,
For bringing him to a sinister scene
So strange, unhomelike, hungry, mean;
His fate the while suspended between

A butcher, to kill out of hand,
And a farmer, to keep on the land;
One can fancy a tear runs down his face
When the butcher wins, and he's driven
     from the place.

THE SUNDIAL ON A WET DAY

I DRIP, drip here
    In Atlantic rain,
Falling like handfuls
Of winnowed grain,
Which, tear-like, down
My gnomon drain,
And dim my numerals
With their stain,—
Till I feel useless,
And wrought in vain!

And then I think
In my despair
That, though unseen,
He is still up there,
And may gaze out
Anywhen, anywhere;
Not to help clockmen
Quiz and compare,
But in kindness to let me
My trade declare.

St. Juliot.

232

HER HAUNTING-GROUND

CAN it be so?   It must be so,
        That visions have not ceased to be
In this the chiefest sanctuary
Of her whose form we used to know.
—Nay, but her dust is far away,
And "where her dust is, shapes her shade,
If spirit clings to flesh," they say:
Yet here her life-parts most were played!

Her voice explored this atmosphere,
Her foot impressed this turf around,
Her shadow swept this slope and mound,
Her fingers fondled blossoms here;
And so, I ask, why, why should she
Haunt elsewhere, by a slighted tomb,
When here she flourished sorrow-free,
And, save for others, knew no gloom?

A PARTING-SCENE

THE two pale women cried,
　　But the man seemed to suffer
　　　more,
　Which he strove hard to hide.
They stayed in the waiting-room, behind
　　the door,
Till startled by the entering engine-roar,
As if they could not bear to have unfurled
Their misery to the eyes of all the world.

　　A soldier and his young wife
　Were the couple; his mother the third,
　　　Who had seen the seams of life.
He was sailing for the East I later heard.
—They kissed long, but they did not speak
　　a word;
Then, strained, he went.　To the elder the
　　wife in tears
"Too long; too long!" burst out.　('Twas
　　for five years.)

SHORTENING DAYS AT THE HOMESTEAD

THE first fire since the summer is lit,
    and is smoking into the room:
The sun-rays thread it through, like
    woof-lines in a loom.
Sparrows spurt from the hedge, whom
    misgivings appal
That winter did not leave last year for ever,
    after all.
    Like shock-headed urchins, spiny-
        haired,
    Stand pollard willows, their twigs just
        bared.

    Who is this coming with pondering
        pace,
    Black and ruddy, with white embossed,
    His eyes being black, and ruddy his
        face,
    And the marge of his hair like morning
        frost?

It's the cider-maker,
And appletree-shaker,
And behind him on wheels, in readi-
ness,
His mill, and tubs, and vat, and press.

DAYS TO RECOLLECT

D^O you recall
That day in Fall
When we walked towards Saint Alban's
Head,
Over thistledown that summer had shed,
Or must I remind you?
Winged thistle-seeds which hitherto
Had lain as none were there, or few,
But rose at the brush of your petticoat-seam
(As ghosts might rise of the recent dead),
And sailed on the breeze in a nebulous
stream
Like a comet's tail behind you:
You don't recall
That day in Fall?

Then do you remember
That sad November
When you left me never to see me more,
And looked quite other than theretofore,
As if it could not *be* you?

And lay by the window whence you had
  gazed
So many times when blamed or praised,
Morning or noon, through years and years,
Accepting the gifts that Fortune bore,
Sharing, enduring, joys, hopes, fears!
  Well: I never more did see you.—
    Say you remember
    That sad November!

TO C. F. H.

FAIR Caroline, I wonder what
    You think of earth as a dwelling-
      spot,
And if you'd rather have come, or not?

To-day has laid on you a name
That, though unasked for, you will claim
Lifelong, for love or praise or blame.

May chance and change impose on you
No heavier burthen than this new
Care-chosen one your future through!

Dear stranger here, the prayer is mine
That your experience may combine
Good things with glad. . . . Yes, Caroline!

THE HIGH-SCHOOL LAWN

GRAY prinked with rose,
    White tipped with blue,
Shoes with gay hose,
Sleeves of chrome hue;
Fluffed frills of white,
Dark bordered light;
Such shimmerings through
Trees of emerald green are eyed
This afternoon, from the road outside.

They whirl around:
Many laughters run
With a cascade's sound;
Then a mere one.

A bell: they flee:
Silence then:——
So it will be
Some day again
With them,——with me.

THE FORBIDDEN BANNS

A BALLAD OF THE EIGHTEEN-THIRTIES

I

"O WHAT'S the gain, my worthy Sir,
    In stopping the banns to-day!
Your son declares he'll marry her
    If a thousand folk say Nay."

"I'll do't; I'll do't; whether or no!
    And, if I drop down dead,
To church this morning I will go,
    And say they shall not wed!"

That day the parson clear outspoke
    The maid's name and the man's:
His father, mid the assembled folk
    Said, "I forbid the banns!"

Then, white in face, lips pale and cold,
    He turned him to sit down,
When he fell forward; and behold,
    They found his life had flown.

II

'Twas night-time, towards the middle part,
    When low her husband said,
"I would from the bottom of my heart
    That father was not dead!"

She turned from one to the other side,
    And a sad woman was she
As he went on: "He'd not have died
    Had it not been for me!"

She brought him soon an idiot child,
    And then she brought another:
His face waned wan, his manner wild
    With hatred of their mother.

"Hearken to me, my son.   No: no:
    There's madness in her blood!"
Those were his father's words; and lo,
    Now, now he understood.

What noise is that?   One noise, and two
    Resound from a near gun.
Two corpses found: and neighbours knew
    By whom the deed was done.

THE PAPHIAN BALL

ANOTHER CHRISTMAS EXPERIENCE OF THE MELLSTOCK QUIRE

WE went our Christmas rounds once
    more,
With quire and viols as theretofore.

Our path was near by Rushy-Pond,
Where Egdon-Heath outstretched beyond.

There stood a figure against the moon,
Tall, spare, and humming a weirdsome
    tune.

"You tire of Christian carols," he said:
"Come and lute at a ball instead.

" 'Tis to your gain, for it ensures
That many guineas will be yours.

"A slight condition hangs on't, true,
But you will scarce say nay thereto:

"That you go blindfold; that anon
The place may not be gossiped on."

They stood and argued with each other:
"Why sing from one house to another

"These   ancient   hymns   in   the   freezing
        night,
And all for nought?   'Tis foolish, quite!"

" —'Tis serving God, and shunning evil:
Might not elsedoing serve the devil?"

"But grand pay!" . . . They were lured
        by his call,
Agreeing to go blindfold all.

They walked, he guiding, some new track,
Doubting to find the pathway back.

In a strange hall they found them when
They were unblinded all again.

Gilded alcoves, great chandeliers,
Voluptuous paintings ranged in tiers.

In brief, a mansion large and rare,
With rows of dancers waiting there.

They tuned and played; the couples
        danced;
Half-naked women tripped, advanced,

With handsome partners footing fast,
Who swore strange oaths, and whirled
        them past.

And thus and thus the slow hours wore
        them:
While shone their guineas heaped before
        them.

Drowsy at length, in lieu of the dance
"*While Shepherds watched . . .*" they
        bowed by chance;

And in a moment, at a blink,
There flashed a change; ere they could
        think

The ball-room vanished and all its crew:
Only the well-known heath they view—

The spot of their crossing overnight,
When wheedled by the stranger's sleight.

There, east, the Christmas dawn hung red,
And dark Rainbarrow with its dead

Bulged like a supine negress' breast
Against Clyffe-Clump's faint far-off crest.

Yea; the rare mansion, gorgeous, bright,
The ladies, gallants, gone were quite.

The heaped-up guineas, too, were gone
With the gold table they were on.

"Why did not grasp we what was owed!"
Cried some, as homeward, shamed, they
    strode.

Now comes the marvel and the warning:
When they had dragged to church next
    morning,

With downcast heads and scarce a word,
They were astound at what they heard.

Praises from all came forth in showers
For how they'd cheered the midnight hours.

"We've heard you many times," friends
    said,
"But like *that* never have you played!

"*Rejoice ye tenants of the earth,*
And celebrate your Saviour's birth,

"Never so thrilled the darkness through,
Or more inspired us so to do!" . . .

—The man who used to tell this tale
Was the tenor-viol, Michael Mail;

Yes; Mail the tenor, now but earth!—
I give it for what it may be worth.

ON MARTOCK MOOR

I

MY deep-dyed husband trusts me,
    He feels his mastery sure,
Although I leave his evening hearth
    To walk upon the moor.

II

—I had what wealth I needed,
    And of gay gowns a score,
And yet I left my husband's house
    To muse upon the moor.

III

O how I loved a dear one
    Who, save in soul, was poor!
O how I loved the man who met
    Me nightly on the moor.

IV

I'd feather-beds and couches,
    And carpets for the floor,
Yet brighter to me was, at eves,
    The bareness of the moor.

V

There was a dogging figure,
    There was a hiss of "Whore!"
There was a flounce at Weir-water
    One night upon the moor. . . .

VI

Yet do I haunt there, knowing
    By rote each rill's low pour,
But only a fitful phantom now
    Meets me upon the moor.

1899.

THAT MOMENT

THE tragedy of that moment
    Was deeper than the sea,
When I came in that moment
    And heard you speak to me!

What I could not help seeing
    Covered life as a blot;
Yes, that which I was seeing,
    And knew that you were not!

PREMONITIONS

"THE bell went heavy to-day
    At afternoon service, they say,
And a screech-owl cried in the boughs,
And a raven flew over the house,
And Betty's old clock with one hand,
That's worn out, as I understand,
And never goes now, never will,
Struck twelve when the night was dead
        still,
Just as when my last loss came to me. . . .
Ah! I wonder who next it will be!

THIS SUMMER AND LAST

UNHAPPY summer you,
  Who do not see
What your yester-summer saw!
Never, never will you be
  Its match to me,
  Never, never draw
  Smiles your forerunner drew,
    Know what it knew!

  Divine things done and said
    Illumined it,
Whose rays crept into corn-brown curls,
Whose breezes heard a humorous wit
    Of fancy flit.—
  Still the alert brook purls,
  Though feet that there would tread
    Elsewhere have sped.

  So, bran-new summer, you
    Will never see
All that yester-summer saw!

252

Never, never will you be
In memory
Its rival, never draw
Smiles your forerunner drew,
Know what it knew!

1913?

"NOTHING MATTERS MUCH"

(B. F. L.)

"NOTHING matters much," he said
Of something just befallen unduly:
He, then active, but now dead,
Truly, truly!

He knew the letter of the law
As voiced by those of wig and gown,
Whose slightest syllogistic flaw
He hammered down.

And often would he shape in word
That nothing needed much lamenting;
And she who sat there smiled and heard,
Sadly assenting.

Facing the North Sea now he lies,
Toward the red altar of the East,
The Flamborough roar his psalmodies,
The wind his priest.

254

And while I think of his bleak bed,
Of Time that builds, of Time that shatters,
Lost to all thought is he, who said
        "Nothing much matters."

IN THE EVENING

IN MEMORIAM FREDERICI TREVES, 1853–1923
(*Dorchester Cemetery, Jan.* 2, 1924)

IN the evening, when the world knew he
      was dead,
    He lay amid the dust and hoar
Of ages; and to a spirit attending said:
      "This chalky bed?—
I surely seem to have been here before?"

"O yes. You have been here. You knew
      the place,
    Substanced as you, long ere your call;
And if you cared to do so you might trace
      In this gray space
Your being, and the being of men all."

Thereto said he: "Then why was I called
      away?
    I knew no trouble or discontent:
Why did I not prolong my ancient stay
      Herein for aye?"
The spirit shook its head. "None knows:
      you went.

"And though, perhaps, Time did not sign
        to you
    The need to go, dream-vision sees
How Aesculapius' phantom hither flew,
            With Galen's, too,
And his of Cos—plague-proof Hippocrates,

"And beckoned you forth, whose skill had
        read as theirs,
    Maybe, had Science chanced to spell
In their day, modern modes to stem despairs
            That mankind bears! . . .
Enough.   You have returned.   And all is
        well."

THE SIX BOARDS

SIX boards belong to me:
    I do not know where they may
      be;
If growing green, or lying dry
    In a cockloft nigh.

Some morning I shall claim them,
And who may then possess will aim them
To bring to me those boards I need
    With thoughtful speed.

But though they hurry so
To yield me mine, I shall not know
How well my want they'll have supplied
    When notified.

Those boards and I—how much
In common we, of feel and touch
Shall share thence on,—earth's far core-
    quakings,
    Hill-shocks, tide-shakings—

Yea, hid where none will note,
The once live tree and man, remote
From mundane hurt as if on Venus, Mars,
Or furthest stars.

BEFORE MY FRIEND ARRIVED

I SAT on the eve-lit weir,
    Which gurgled in sobs and sighs;
I looked across the meadows near
    To the towered church on the rise.
    Overmuch cause had my look!
    I pulled out pencil and book,
    And drew a white chalk mound,
    Outthrown on the sepulchred ground.

    Why did I pencil that chalk?
    It was fetched from the waiting grave,
    And would return there soon,
    Of one who had stilled his walk
    And sought oblivion's cave.
He was to come on the morrow noon
And take a good rest in the bed so hewn.

He came, and there he is now, although
This was a wondrous while ago.
And the sun still dons a ruddy dye;
    The weir still gurgles nigh;
    The tower is dark on the sky.

COMPASSION

AN ODE

IN CELEBRATION OF THE CENTENARY OF THE ROYAL
SOCIETY FOR THE PREVENTION OF CRUELTY TO
ANIMALS

I

BACKWARD among the dusky years
    A lonesome lamp is seen arise,
Lit by a few fain pioneers
    Before incredulous eyes.—
We read the legend that it lights:
"Wherefore beholds this land of historied
    rights
Mild creatures, despot-doomed, bewildered,
    plead
Their often hunger, thirst, pangs, prison-
    ment,
    In deep dumb gaze more eloquent
        Than tongues of widest heed?"

II

What was faint-written, read in a breath
In that year—ten times ten away—

A larger louder conscience saith
    More sturdily to-day.—
But still those innocents are thralls
To throbless hearts, near, far, that hear no
    calls
Of honour towards their too-dependent
    frail,
And from Columbia Cape to Ind we see
    How helplessness breeds tyranny
        In power above assail.

III

Cries still are heard in secret nooks,
    Till hushed with gag or slit or thud;
And hideous dens whereon none looks
        Are sprayed with needless blood.
But here, in battlings, patient, slow,
Much has been won—more, maybe, than
    we know—
And on we labour hopeful. "Ailinon!"
A mighty voice calls: "But may the good
    prevail!"
    And "Blessed are the merciful!"
        Calls a yet mightier one.

January 22, 1924.

"WHY SHE MOVED HOUSE"

(THE DOG MUSES)

WHY she moved house, without a
          word,
  I cannot understand;
She'd mirrors, flowers, she'd book and
      bird,
  And callers in a band.

And where she is she gets no sun,
  No flowers, no book, no glass;
Of callers I am the only one,
  And I but pause and pass.

TRAGEDIAN TO TRAGEDIENNE

SHALL I leave you behind me
    When I play
In earnest what we've played in mock to-
    day?

Why, yes; most surely shall I
    Leave you behind
In yet full orbit, when my years unwind.

I may creep off in the night-time,
    And none know
Till comes the morning, bringing news 'tis
    so.

Will you then turn for a moment
    White or red,
Recall those spells of ours; things done,
    things said?

Aye, those adventurous doings
    And those days
Of stress, when I'd the blame and you the
    praise?

Still you will meet adventure—
　　　　None knows what—
Still you will go on changing: I shall not.

Still take a call at the mummings
　　　　Daily or nightly,
Yielding to custom, calmly, gloomily,
　　brightly.

Last, you will flag, and finish
　　　　Your masquings too:
Yes: end them: I not there to succour you.

THE LADY OF FOREBODINGS

"WHAT do you so regard, my lady,
            Sitting beside me here?
    Are there not days as clear
As this to come, ev'n shaped less shady?"
"O no," said she. "Come what delight
        To you, by voice or pen,
To me will fall such day, such night,
            Not, not again!"

The lamps above and round were fair,
        The tables were aglee,
        As if 'twould ever be
That we should smile and sit on there.
But yet she said, as though she must,
        "Yes: it will soon be gone,
And all its dearness leave but dust
            To muse upon."

THE BIRD-CATCHER'S BOY

"FATHER, I fear your trade:
　　Surely it's wrong!
Little birds limed and made
　　Captive life-long.

"Larks bruise and bleed in jail,
　　Trying to rise;
Every caged nightingale
　　Soon pines and dies."

"Don't be a dolt, my boy!
　　Birds must be caught;
My lot is such employ,
　　Yours to be taught.

"Soft shallow stuff as that
　　Out from your head!
Just learn your lessons pat,
　　Then off to bed."

Lightless, without a word
   Bedwise he fares;
Groping his way is heard
   Seek the dark stairs

Through the long passage, where
   Hang the caged choirs:
Harp-like his fingers there
   Sweep on the wires.

Next day, at dye of dawn,
   Freddy was missed:
Whither the boy had gone
   Nobody wist.

That week, the next one, whiled:
   No news of him:
Weeks up to months were piled:
   Hope dwindled dim.

Yet not a single night
   Locked they the door,
Waiting, heart-sick, to sight
   Freddy once more.

Hopping there long anon
   Still the birds hung:
Like those in Babylon
   Captive, they sung.

One wintry Christmastide
   Both lay awake;
All cheer within them dried,
   Each hour an ache.

Then some one seemed to flit
   Soft in below;
"Freddy's come!"   Up they sit
   Faces aglow.

Thereat a groping touch
   Dragged on the wires
Lightly and softly—much
   As they were lyres;

"Just as it used to be
   When he came in,
Feeling in darkness the
   Stairway to win!"

Waiting a trice or two
   Yet, in the gloom,
Both parents pressed into
   Freddy's old room.

There on the empty bed
   White the moon shone,
As ever since they'd said,
   "Freddy is gone!"

270 THE BIRD-CATCHER'S BOY

That night at Durdle-Door *
Foundered a hoy,
And the tide washed ashore
One sailor boy.

November 21, 1912.

* Durdle-Door, a rock on the south coast.

A HURRIED MEETING

IT is August moonlight in the tall plan-
tation,
Whose elms, by aged squirrels' footsteps
worn,
  Outscreen the noon, and eve, and morn.
On the facing slope a faint irradiation
  From a mansion's marble front is borne,
    Mute in its woodland wreathing.
  Up here the night-jar whirrs forlorn,
And the trees seem to withhold their softest
breathing.

To the moonshade slips a woman in muslin
vesture:
Her naked neck the gossamer-web besmears,
  And she sweeps it away with a hasty
gesture.
Again it touches her forehead, her neck, her
ears,

Her fingers, the backs of her hands.
She sweeps it away again
　　Impatiently, and then
She takes no notice; and listens, and sighs,
　　and stands.

The night-hawk stops.　A man shows in
　　the obscure:
　　They meet, and passively kiss,
And he says: "Well, I've come quickly.
　　About this—
　　Is it really so?　You are sure?"
"I am sure.　In February it will be.
That such a thing should come to me!
We should have known.　We should have
　　left off meeting.
Love is a terrible thing: a sweet allure
　　That ends in heart-outeating!"

　　"But what shall we do, my Love, and
　　how?"
　　"You need not call me by that name
　　now."
Then he more coldly: "What is your
　　suggestion?"
"I've told my mother, and she sees a way,
Since of our marriage there can be no
　　question.
We are crossing South—near about New
　　Year's Day

The event will happen there.
It is the only thing that we can dare
    To keep them unaware!"
    "Well, you can marry me."
She shook her head. "No: that can never be.

" 'Twill be brought home as hers. She's
        forty-one,
When many a woman's bearing is not
        done,
    And well might have a son.—
We should have left off specious self-
        deceiving:
    I feared that such might come,
    And knowledge struck me numb.
Love is a terrible thing: witching when
        first begun,
    To end in grieving, grieving!"

And with one kiss again the couple parted:
Inferior clearly he; she haughty-hearted.
He watched her down the slope to return to
        her place,
The marble mansion of her ancient race,
And saw her brush the gossamers from her
        face
As she emerged from shade to the moon-
        light ray.

And when she had gone away
The night-jar seemed to imp, and say,
"You should have taken warning:
Love is a terrible thing: sweet for a space,
And then all mourning, mourning!"

DISCOURAGEMENT

TO see the Mother, naturing Nature,
     stand
All racked and wrung by her unfaithful
     lord,
Her hopes dismayed by his defiling hand,
Her passioned plans for bloom and beauty
     marred.

Where she would mint a perfect mould, an
     ill;
Where she would don divinest hues, a stain,
Over her purposed genial hour a chill,
Upon her charm of flawless flesh a blain:

Her loves dependent on a feature's trim,
A whole life's circumstance on hap of birth,
A soul's direction on a body's whim,
Eternal Heaven upon a day of Earth,
Is frost to flower of heroism and worth,
And fosterer of visions ghast and grim.

Westbourne Park Villas, 1863-7.
          (From old MS.)

A LEAVING

KNOWING what it bore
        I watched the rain-smitten
back of the car—
(Brown-curtained, such as the old ones
        were)—
    When it started forth for a journey afar
  Into the sullen November air,
And passed the glistening laurels and round
        the bend.

I have seen many gayer vehicles turn that
        bend
    In autumn, winter, and summer air,
    Bearing for journeys near or afar
    Many who now are not, but were,
    But I don't forget that rain-smitten car,
        Knowing what it bore!

SONG TO AN OLD BURDEN

THE feet have left the wormholed
        flooring,
    That danced to the ancient air,
    The fiddler, all-ignoring,
Sleeps by the gray-grassed 'cello player:
Shall I then foot around around around,
    As once I footed there!

The voice is heard in the room no longer
    That trilled, none sweetlier,
    To gentle stops or stronger,
Where now the dust-draped cobwebs stir:
Shall I then sing again again again,
    As once I sang with her!

The eyes that beamed out rapid brightness
    Have longtime found their close,
    The cheeks have wanned to whiteness
That used to sort with summer rose:
Shall I then joy anew anew anew,
    As once I joyed in those!

278 SONG TO AN OLD BURDEN

O what's to me this tedious Maying,
 What's to me this June?
 O why should viols be playing
To catch and reel and rigadoon?
Shall I sing, dance around around around,
 When phantoms call the tune!

"WHY DO I?"

WHY do I go on doing these things?
          Why not cease?
Is it that you are yet in this world of
          welterings
          And unease,
And that, while so, mechanic repetitions
          please?

     When shall I leave off doing these
          things?—
          When I hear
You have dropped your dusty cloak and
          taken you wondrous wings
          To another sphere,
Where no pain is: Then shall I hush this
          dinning gear.